KU-035-313

# CONTENTS

| | | | |
|---|---|---|---|
| Preface | | | 6 |
| Climbing in North Wales | | | 7 |
| How to use the Guide | | | 8 |

**Ogwen Area**

| | | | | |
|---|---|---|---|---|
| 1 | Amphitheatre Buttress | Craig yr Ysfa | VD | 20 |
| 2 | Mur y Niwl/Pinnacle Wall | Craig yr Ysfa | VS+ | 22 |
| 3 | W Great Gully | Craig yr Ysfa | S or IV | 24 |
| 4 | The Groove | Llech Du | E1 | 26 |
| 5 | W Western Gully | Black Ladders | IV | 28 |
| 6 | W Northern Ridges | Tryfan & Glyder Fach | E or I/II | 30 |
| 7 | Direct Route | Milestone Buttress | VD | 32 |
| 8 | Soapgut/Chimney Route | Milestone Buttress | VS | 34 |
| 9 | Grooved Arete | Tryfan – East Face | VD+ | 36 |
| 10 | Pinnacle Rib | Tryfan – East Face | VD+ | 38 |
| 11 | Gashed Crag | Tryfan – East Face | VD+ | 40 |
| | Munich | Tryfan – East Face | VS | 40 |
| 12 | Bochlwyd Main Face | Bochlwyd Buttress | VD+, S+, HVS | 42 |
| 13 | W Central Gully | Glyder Fach | II/III | 44 |
| 14 | Chasm Route | Glyder Fach | VD+ | 46 |
| 15 | Direct Route | Glyder Fach | S or VS | 48 |
| 16 | Lot's Groove | Glyder Fach | VS+ | 49 |
| | Lot's Wife | Glyder Fach | VS | 49 |
| 17 | Gribin Classics | Gribin Facet | D, S or VS | 50 |
| 18 | Ordinary/Cneifion Arete | Idwal/Cneifion | D | 52 |
| 19 | Faith | Idwal Slabs & Walls | VD | 54 |
| | Hope | Idwal Slabs & Walls | VD | 54 |
| | Charity | Idwal Slabs & Walls | VD | 54 |
| 20 | East Wall Girdle | Idwal Slabs & Walls | S+ | 56 |
| 21 | Holly Tree Wall | Idwal Slabs & Walls | VS | 58 |
| 22 | Suicide Wall | Idwal Slabs & Walls | E2 | 60 |
| 23 | Grey Slab | Idwal Slabs & Walls | VS | 62 |
| | Grey Arete | Idwal Slabs & Walls | HVS | 62 |
| 24 | W Clogwyn Du Gully | Clogwyn Du | III or IV | 64 |
| 25 | W South Gully | Devil's Kitchen | IV | 66 |
| 26 | W The Ramp | Devil's Kitchen | II/III | 68 |
| | W The Screen | Devil's Kitchen | IV | 68 |
| 27 | Devil's Kitchen | Devil's Kitchen | VD+ | 70 |
| | Devil's Staircase | Devil's Kitchen | S | 70 |

**Llanberis Pass Area**

| | | | | |
|---|---|---|---|---|
| 28 | Brant | Clogwyn y Grochan | VS | 76 |
| | Brant Direct | Clogwyn y Grochan | VS+ | 76 |
| 29 | Nea | Clogwyn y Grochan | S+ | 78 |
| 30 | Spectre | Clogwyn y Grochan | HVS | 80 |
| 31 | Wrinkle | Carreg Wastad | VD | 81 |
| 32 | Crackstone Rib | Carreg Wastad | S | 82 |
| 33 | Flying Buttress | Dinas Cromlech | D+ | 84 |
| 34 | Cemetery Gates | Dinas Cromlech | E1 | 86 |

| 35 | Cenotaph Corner | Dinas Cromlech | E1 | 88 |
| 36 | Left Wall | Dinas Cromlech | E2 | 89 |
| 37 | Dives/Better Things | Dinas Cromlech | S+ | 90 |
| 38 | The Cracks/Slow Ledge | Dinas Mot | S+ | 92 |
| 39 | Direct Route | Dinas Mot | VS | 94 |
| 40 | Diagonal | Dinas Mot | HVS | 96 |
| | Superdirect | Dinas Mot | E1 | 96 |
| 41 | The Mole/Gollum | Dinas Mot | HVS | 98 |
| 42 | Plexus | Dinas Mot | HVS | 100 |
| 43 | Main Wall | Cyrn Las | S+ | 102 |
| 44 | The Grooves | Cyrn Las | E1 | 104 |
| 45 | W Parsley Fern Gully | Clogwyn y Ddysgl | I or II | 105 |
| 46 | Gambit Climb | Clogwyn y Ddysgl | VD+ | 106 |

**Snowdon Area**

| 47 | W Snowdon Horseshoe | Snowdon | E or I/II | 112 |
| 48 | Slanting Buttress | Lliwedd | D | 114 |
| 49 | Horned Crag | Lliwedd | VD+ | 116 |
| 50 | Route II/Red Wall | Lliwedd | S | 118 |
| 51 | W Trinity Face Routes | Clogwyn y Garnedd | I to III | 120 |
| 52 | The Mostest | Clogwyn Du'r Arddu | E2 | 122 |
| 53 | Shrike | Clogwyn Du'r Arddu | E1 | 124 |
| 54 | Llithrig/Pinnacle Arete | Clogwyn Du'r Arddu | E1 | 126 |
| 55 | Pigott's Climb | Clogwyn Du'r Arddu | VS+ | 128 |
| | Chimney Route | Clogwyn Du'r Arddu | VS | 128 |
| 56 | Curving Crack | Clogwyn Du'r Arddu | VS | 130 |
| | Vember | Clogwyn Du'r Arddu | E1 | 130 |
| 57 | Pedestal Crack Direct | Clogwyn Du'r Arddu | VS+ | 132 |
| | The Corner | Clogwyn Du'r Arddu | HVS | 132 |
| 58 | The Boulder | Clogwyn Du'r Arddu | HVS | 133 |
| 59 | Longland's Climb | Clogwyn Du'r Arddu | VS | 134 |
| 60 | White Slab | Clogwyn Du'r Arddu | E1 | 136 |
| | West Butt. Eliminate | Clogwyn Du'r Arddu | E2 | 136 |
| 61 | Great/Bow Combination | Clogwyn Du'r Arddu | VS+ | 138 |
| 62 | Oxine | Clogwyn y Wenallt | VS+ | 140 |

**Outlying Areas**

| 63 | Lavaredo | Carreg Alltrem | VS+ | 146 |
| | Lightning Visit | Carreg Alltrem | VS | 146 |
| 64 | Asahel/Eagle Finish | Moelwyns – Clipiau | VS | 148 |
| 65 | Mean Feet | Moelwyns – Clipiau | VS+ | 150 |
| 66 | Y Gelynen | Moelwyns – Wrysgan | S | 152 |
| 67 | Kirkus's Climb Direct | Moelwyns – Oen | VD+ | 154 |
| 68 | Slick | Moelwyns – Oen | VD | 156 |
| | Slack | Moelwyns – Oen | S | 156 |
| 69 | Dwm | Castell Cidwm | HVS/A1 | 158 |
| 70 | Ordinary Route | Cwm Silyn – Craig yr Ogof | D | 160 |
| | Outside Edge | Cwm Silyn – Craig yr Ogof | VD+ | 160 |

# 100 CLASSIC CLIMBS

# NORTH WALES

## Steve Ashton

The Crowood Press

First published in 1988 by
The Crowood Press Ltd
Ramsbury, Marlborough
Wiltshire SN8 2HR

This impression 1995

© Steve Ashton 1988

All rights reserved. No part of this publication may be reproduced or
transmitted in any form or by any means, electronic or mechanical, including
photocopy, recording, or any information storage and retrieval system without
permisssion in writing from the publishers.

British Library Cataloguing in Publication Data

Ashton, Steve
    100 classic climbs in North Wales.
    1. Wales, North – Description and travel – Guide books
    I. Title
    914.29'104858    DA740.N6

    ISBN 1 85223 020 7

**Acknowledgements**

These climbs were shared with friends. I owe them my thanks: Shân Ashton,
Tony Ashton, Dave Baines, Eddie Birch, Marion Brogan, Jim Buckley, Olly
Burrows, Mike Combley, John Cousins, Malc Creasey, Alan Davies, Rob
Eagle, Pete Evans, Chris French, Dave Hardy, John Jackson, Jethro Jeffrey,
Crag Jones, Dave Knighton, Richard Leigh, Mary MacKenzie, Barry Owen,
Bill Parker, Dave Paxton, Alan Pinder, Stephan Reid, Terry Storry, Tom
Walkington, Pauline Wharrad, Joc White, Dave Whiting, Dave Williams, Paul
Williams, Bern Woodhouse, John Young. Thanks also to John Sumner for
providing details of some Central Wales routes.

Printed in Great Britain by The Bath Press

| 71 | Kirkus's Direct | Cwm Silyn – Craig yr Ogof | VS+ | 162 |
| 72 | Crucible | Cwm Silyn – Craig yr Ogof | HVS | 164 |
| | Jabberwocky | Cwm Silyn – Craig yr Ogof | E2 | 164 |
| 73 | Cyfrwy Arete | Cader Idris – Cyfrwy | D | 166 |
| | Rib and Slab | Cader Idris – Cyfrwy | S+ | 166 |
| 74 | W Great Gully | Cader Idris – Craig Cau | III/IV | 168 |
| 75 | Aardvark | Aran – Gist Ddu | HVS | 170 |
| 76 | Acheron | Aran – Craig Cywarch | VS+ | 172 |
| 77 | W Maesglasau Falls | Aran – Craig Maesglasau | IV | 174 |

**Coastal Areas**

| 78 | Britomartis | Gogarth – Wen Zawn | VS+ | 180 |
| | Spider Wall | Gogarth – Wen Zawn | HVS | 180 |
| 79 | A Dream of White Horses | Gogarth – Wen Zawn | HVS | 182 |
| 80 | Wen | Gogarth – Wen Zawn | VS+ | 184 |
| | Concrete Chimney | Gogarth – Wen Zawn | HVS | 184 |
| 81 | Gogarth | Gogarth – Main Cliff | E1 | 186 |
| 82 | Central Park | Gogarth – Upper Tier | VS+ | 188 |
| | The Strand | Gogarth – Upper Tier | E1 | 188 |
| 83 | Mousetrap | Gogarth – South Stack | E1 | 190 |
| 84 | Red Wall | Gogarth – South Stack | E1 | 192 |
| 85 | Blanco | Gogarth – South Stack | HVS | 194 |
| 86 | True Moments/Freebird | Gogarth – South Stack | E2 | 196 |
| 87 | Tensor | Tremadog – Castell | HVS | 197 |
| | The Wasp | Tremadog – Castell | E1 | 197 |
| 88 | Creagh Dhu Wall | Tremadog – Castell | S+ | 198 |
| 89 | Poor Man's Peuterey | Tremadog – Pant Ifan | S+ | 200 |
| 90 | Pincushion | Tremadog – Pant Ifan | HVS | 202 |
| | Barbarian | Tremadog – Pant Ifan | HVS | 202 |
| 91 | Scratch | Tremadog – Pant Ifan | VS | 204 |
| | Scratch Arete | Tremadog – Pant Ifan | VS+ | 204 |
| 92 | Falcon | Tremadog – Pant Ifan | E1 | 206 |
| 93 | Christmas Curry | Tremadog | S or S+ | 208 |
| | The Plum | Tremadog | E1 | 208 |
| 94 | The Fang | Tremadog | HVS | 210 |
| | Extraction | Tremadog | E2 | 210 |
| | Striptease | Tremadog | VS+ | 210 |
| 95 | One Step in the Clouds | Tremadog | VS | 212 |
| 96 | Vector | Tremadog | E2 | 214 |
| | The Weaver | Tremadog | E2 | 214 |
| 97 | Meshach | Tremadog | VS+ | 216 |
| | Shadrach | Tremadog | VS | 216 |
| 98 | Leg Slip | Tremadog | HVS | 218 |
| | First Slip | Tremadog | E1 | 218 |
| 99 | Merlin | Tremadog | S | 220 |
| | Merlin Direct | Tremadog | VS+ | 220 |
| 100 | Hardd | Carreg Hylldrem | E1 | 222 |
| | Hylldrem Girdle | Carreg Hylldrem | VS+ | 222 |

# Preface

This guide selects classic rock and ice climbs from North Wales and describes them in a new way. Topo diagrams take the place of formal route descriptions, while an accompanying text explores the special quality and atmosphere of the routes. Through this approach, route finding reverts to its more natural and adventurous origins.

*100 Classic Climbs* has a fine ring to it for a book title, but strictly speaking it is inaccurate. In some instances two or three routes have been clustered under one heading. As a result the actual number of routes you can find and follow from this guide is closer to 200. Nevertheless, only a fraction of the several thousand climbs in North Wales could be included.

About half of the routes chose themselves. I am confident that no one will question the inclusion of Grooved Arête, Cenotaph Corner, Main Wall, White Slab, and the fifty or so other routes of comparable status.

Defining a range of admissible grades also helped to trim the selection. There is no lower limit, while the upper limit stops short of *E3*. More *Extremes* would have meant fewer *Diffs* and *Severes*, which I felt would have been unacceptable to the majority of users. This also explains the exclusion of coastal limestone and quarried slate.

From the outset I was determined to include at least a dozen winter routes. As it is, most of the classics have been included in one form or another. The upper limit stops short of grade *V*, the relative infrequency of suitable conditions on these routes being a contributory factor. NOTE: Pegs come and go on these routes and those indicated on the topo diagrams are *probably*, not *necessarily*, in situ. Please don't assume they will be in place or in a usable condition during your ascent.

With the classic core of the book established, it was then a matter of strengthening the selection in certain areas – the object being to describe sufficient routes at each major crag for a full day's climbing. A few remaining spaces were then filled with personal favourites, for which I make no apology. I hope you like them too.

# Climbing in North Wales

A rich variety of climbing puts North Wales ahead of all rival venues. In no other region is this mix of mountain and lowland rock available in such compact and accessible form.

Ogwen is the best base for novices and mountaineers. Popular valley crags include the Milestone Buttress and Idwal Slabs. Unfortunately their holds are badly polished, which detracts from the degree of security – actual and perceived. The scope for mountaineering is tremendous. A favourite place in summer is the East Face of Tryfan, where long rock climbs lead to the finest summit in Wales. In winter the experienced mountaineer can choose between remote Carneddau gullies and accessible Idwal ice-falls.

Ogwen has its share of difficult climbs, but the greatest concentration will be found in and around the Llanberis Pass. Those on its sunny north side are extremely popular, not least because of a fifteen minute approach. This style of climbing reaches its ultimate expression on the central walls of Dinas Cromlech. In the shade opposite, on Dinas Mot, will be found a greater diversity of climbing. This includes *Extreme* slab climbing as well as the usual acrobatics on vertical rock.

Both styles of climbing come together on Clogwyn Du'r Arddu, centre-piece of the Snowdon area and the finest cliff in the country. Notable climbs are *VS* or harder, but the history mapped out on these sombre walls touches all rock climbers. Mountain rock on Lliwedd, and snow gullies on Clogwyn y Garnedd, reset the balance.

Outlying areas contain pockets of both outcrop and mountain rock. All standards are represented, although concentrations of each are too scattered to make a base here worthwhile. Fortunately all lie within daily travelling distance of central regions.

Coastal cliffs at Tremadog and Gogarth are a tremendous asset to North Wales climbing, their mild climates justifying a weekend visit during doubtful weather or out of season. More than that, both areas offer superb climbing in their own right. Most of it is in the higher grades, but there are a handful of *Severes* at Tremadog which rank with the best.

# How to use the Guide

## AREA INTRODUCTIONS

Routes are described under one of five area headings: Ogwen, Llanberis Pass, Snowdon, Outlying and Coastal. A brief introduction to each describes climbing typical of the area, and highlights major crags. Further notes identify approaches by car or public transport, and suggest where to look for accommodation. An accompanying map locates valley bases, parking places, and crag approach paths.

## ROUTE INFORMATION

Concise details of each route are presented under six headings:

**Summary:** A short appraisal of the route for quick reference purposes. Along with route grade and length, this tells you all you need to know when looking for ideas.

**First Ascent:** These names and dates are of little immediate significance but add historical perspective.

**Best Conditions:** Helps you find a suitable route according to the season and prevailing weather – hot, cold, dry, or wet.

**Approach:** Gets you to the crag with a minimum of fuss. Provides concise information on parking, as well as on the approach route and its duration. Grid references refer to the relevant Ordnance Survey map (use this reminder to check calculations if you forget the reference convention: Snowdon Summit is at GR.610 544).

**Starting Point:** Locates the start and fixes the beginning of the topo, from which all further directions will be taken. Refer to crag diagrams or prominent features shown on the topo if you need to confirm position.

**Descent:** Briefly describes the most common descent routes (which are also indicated on topos and crag diagrams).

## ROUTE DESCRIPTIONS

The half page of 'chat' following summarised route information is something you might read in the campsite or pub, rather than on the crag. Its purpose is to sketch in a background to the climb. Rarely will it contain information essential for route finding – that is the role of the topo. However, if you get badly stuck you might find the odd clue secreted here!

## TOPO DIAGRAMS

For simplicity, all routes are identified by a number from 1 to 100. These numbers are used consistently throughout the text as well as on topos, crag diagrams and area maps.

Topos take the place of formal route descriptions; you will be surprised how quickly you learn to 'read' the route by interpreting these symbols. A key at the rear of the book explains what they mean.

Most topos have been based on photographs, so relative distances between stances and other features should be reasonably accurate. They have been corrected for gross foreshortening, except when the effect aids identification during the approach (a note on the diagram makes this clear). *Warning*: Don't read too much into each little twist and kink of the dotted line. The same applies to distance scales. Topos can only show the *approximate* line of a route and are best used as confirmation of intuitive route-finding decisions.

A few topos serve clusters of two or three routes. Numbering makes it plain which is which. In some cases a worthwhile neighbouring route has been indicated. Absence of a number confirms that there will be no further elaboration in the text.

## GRADINGS

Nothing too controversial here. Normal adjectival grades, suitably abbreviated, have been used throughout, with the addition of a *VS+* grade to ease congestion in the *VS* and *HVS* grades.

Technical grades appear directly on the topos, pinpointing major difficulties. The full range of grades, and their approximate international equivalents, are as follows:

| British Adjectival Grade | | Technical | UIAA | USA |
|---|---|---|---|---|
| E | Easy | | I | |
| M | Moderate | | II | |
| D | Difficult | | III− | |
| D+ | Hard Difficult | | III | |
| VD | Very Difficult | | III+ | |
| VD+ | Hard Very Difficult | | IV | |
| S | Severe | | IV+ | |
| S+ | Hard Severe | 4a, *4b*, 4c | V | 5.6 |
| VS | Very Severe | 4b, *4c*, 5a | V+ | 5.7 |
| VS+ | Very Severe (hard) | *4c, 5a* | VI− | 5.8 |
| HVS | Hard Very Severe | 4c, *5a*, 5b | VI | 5.9 |
| E1 | Mild Extremely Severe | 5a, *5b*, 5c | VI+/VII− | 5.10a/b |
| E2 | Extremely Severe | 5b, *5c*, 6a | VII | 5.10c/d |

**Interpreting Grades:** The adjectival, or overall, grade takes into account the seriousness of a route as well as its pure technical difficulty. However, the range of technical difficulties likely to be encountered at a given overall grade is limited. This range is indicated on the table (the most common grade is italicised). An unusual combination of adjectival and technical grade reveals a great deal about the route. Consider the Direct Route (*VS, 5b*) and Mousetrap (*E1, 5a*). From these particular combinations we assume, correctly as it happens, that major technical difficulties on the Direct will be comparatively short and safe, whereas those on Mousetrap will be prolonged and serious.

**Regional Variations:** Grading attempts to be consistent across all five areas, but discrepancies remain. For instance, you may find yourself having to work a lot harder at Tremadog than you would at Gogarth to succeed on a route of the same grade. A friendlier atmosphere at Tremadog lends itself to struggle, so perhaps there is some justification. Similar arguments could be used to explain other inconsistencies. Nevertheless, it is always a good idea to drop down a grade when first visiting a new area.

Take extra care when relating these grades to those used in other parts of Britain. In a grade for grade comparison, Lake District climbs will seem about the same; Scottish rock, and Peak and Pennine limestone rather more difficult; and Peak and Pennine grit, at least in purely technical terms, distinctly brutal.

**Aid Climbing:** Aid routes are graded on a separate system from *A1* to *A5* in increasing order of difficulty and seriousness. Only one route in this selection – Dwm (Route 69) – includes a substantial amount of aid climbing, and then at a lowly *A1* grade requiring no special equipment or technique. Traditional aid points have been retained in some cases, despite the fact that all routes in the book have been climbed completely free. Otherwise we would have lost White Slab, Llithrig, Tensor and Pincushion.

**Star Ratings:** Star ratings to indicate route quality would have been superfluous in this guide – they are all excellent!

# WINTER ROUTES

If you are contemplating winter climbing for the first time, please take advice and instruction beforehand on equipment and techniques. This guide describes only where to find the routes, not how to climb them or how to stay alive in the hostile winter environment.

**Snow & Ice Conditions:** North Wales produces the best winter climbing outside Scotland. That statement is not quite so encouraging as it sounds; mild weather arriving mid-season can completely strip the hillsides of snow and ice – something that never happens in Scotland. Powder snow and brittle ice offer poor support and increase avalanche risk during the early stages of a cold period; wet snow and rotten ice do the same at the onset of thaw. The best snow conditions arrive when night frosts harden the surface of old snow, whereas the best water ice often occurs during the transitional period between intense cold and thaw. Sadly the snow-ice found at higher altitudes in Scotland is rarely encountered in North Wales.

**Grading:** Winter routes are identified in the contents list by a (*W*). They have been graded according to the familiar Scottish system, with slight modifications to suit Welsh conditions:

I Simple snow gullies, possibly including a small ice step or corniced exit. Uncomplicated ridge traverses under good conditions.

II Snow gullies containing a few small pitches. Exposed ridges which include small rock steps and/or knife-edges.

III Gullies containing several pitches, some of which may be long or problematical. Escapable or low-angle ice-falls (frozen stream courses, for example).

IV Major gullies containing several difficult pitches. Steep ice-falls of continuous difficulty.

V Major gullies with additional difficulties such as technical rock sections. Ice-falls which include long vertical sections.

In some cases a borderline grade has been allocated (for example *III/IV*). This is self explanatory. All grades relate to good winter conditions, so expect dramatic increases in difficulty if these deteriorate.

**Equipment:** Grades assume that twin tools will be used on all but the simplest outings, and that for ice routes these will have inclined or steeply drooped picks. Special mention has usually been made when screws or deadmen (or buried axes) are essential for belaying. Four or five pegs and a small selection of nuts and slings are normally carried on routes graded *III* or harder.

Other essential winter equipment includes: helmet (a must on ice-falls!), spare food and clothing for enforced bivouacs, head-torch with spare bulb and battery, survival bag, spare mitts, map and compass.

**Timing:** Monitor weather and ground conditions and set out early to get the best from North Wales winter climbing. Your reward will be smaller queues, optimum conditions, fewer benightments, and a longer life.

# ACCESS

Crag approaches follow paths which are in regular use. However, there is no automatic right of access. Discretion and courtesy – coupled with a quiet determination to succeed – are most likely to get results if problems arise in sensitive areas such as Aran, Rhyd Ddu and Tremadog.

# METRIC UNITS

Metric units have been used throughout. Metric Ordnance Survey maps justify conversion of distances and heights, while metric ropes partially excuse conversion of route lengths. Incorrigible imperialists can reconvert by adding a zero and dividing by three (60m=600/3=200ft – actual conversion slightly under 197ft). Alternatively, for a rough approximation, multiply by three and then add a bit for good measure (a tenth to be more precise).

# MORE INFORMATION

**Maps:** Ordnance Survey maps are useful for locating crags, and essential when planning a mountain day. Routes 1–72 are conveniently shown on the 1:50,000 Snowdon Area map (OS Sheet 115). Tremadog, Cader Idris and Aran routes are shown on the 1:50,000 Dolgellau map (Sheet 124). Additionally, a 1:25,000 scale map is worth having for Snowdon and Ogwen areas. Number 17 (Snowdon) in the OS 'Outdoor Leisure' series includes the important bits of both areas. A map for Gogarth is not really necessary.

**Comprehensive Guidebooks:** The Climbers' Club publish a series of comprehensive guides to rock climbs in North Wales. These are most useful once regular visits have begun to exhaust the possibilities contained in this guide. At present the series consists of nine volumes.

# EMERGENCIES
## First Aid Checklist

**Check Breathing**
- If necessary clear airway using a hooked finger to remove obstructions – vomit, blood, teeth etc.
- Turn casualty to lie in the recovery position (unless you suspect spinal injury). This helps to maintain a clear airway.

**Check For Severe Bleeding**
- Apply direct pressure from a pad to stop bleeding.
- Elevate the limb.

**Check For Broken Bones**
- Do not move the casualty if a spinal injury is suspected.
- Immobilise other fractures using improvised splints and slings.

**Monitor Condition**
- Keep casualty warm and comfortable while awaiting rescue (protect from wind and insulate from cold ground).
- Reassure casualty and monitor condition regularly.

**To Alert Mountain Rescue**
Dial 999, ask for police (mountain rescue), and try to have the following written details ready:
- Name and description of injured person.
- Precise position of the injured person on the crag.
- Location of the crag (including *grid reference* and *map sheet number*).
- Time and nature of accident.
- Extent of injuries.
- Indication of prevailing weather at the scene (cloud base, wind strength, visibility, etc.).
- Remain by the phone until met by a police officer or member of the rescue team.

**Rescue Helicopters**
- Secure all loose equipment before arrival of helicopter (weight rucksacks, jackets etc. with stones).
- Identify yourself by raising your arms in a V as helicopter approaches. Do *not* wave.
- Protect injured person from rotor downdraught (which is intense).
- Allow winchman to land of his own accord.
- Do not approach helicopter unless directed to do so by one of the crew (danger from rotors, exhaust, etc.).

# A FINAL CAUTIONARY NOTE

A guidebook of this sort reflects the author's own reactions and responses to the routes. Not everyone will agree on the exact lines to follow, the levels of difficulty encountered, or the best techniques to apply. Route information has been based on notes and sketches produced while at the crag or shortly afterwards. Nevertheless, when faced by an unexpected route finding problem ultimately you would be wise to trust your own intuition.

Possible author errors are not the only reason to stay alert; dramatic changes can take place on the rock itself. Several pitches were altered or destroyed during the writing of this guide (Merlin, Nea and Superdirect spring to mind). In each case the route was reclimbed by its new line and the necessary alterations made to the text. However, there is no reason to suppose that trees will cease to wither, ledges erode, or buttresses collapse, in the intervening period between this book going to press and your reading of it.

If you *do* experience any difficulty because of an error on my part (for I which I apologise, most sincerely, in advance), or because of changes to the crag itself, or indeed if you have any other comments on the guide, then please write to Steve Ashton care of The Crowood Press. I would be very grateful, and your help in updating the guide would be acknowledged in future revisions.

# Ogwen Area

Without doubt, the most satisfying Ogwen days are based around one of the long mountaineering routes. The distribution of climbs chosen to represent the Glyders reflects this strength. Although the neighbouring Carneddau have been allocated relatively little space, the routes chosen rank alongside the very best in Wales.

Ogwen, along with Snowdon, can boast the most reliable winter climbing south of Scotland. The Carneddau area distinguishes itself again with two great gullies, while the Kitchen Cliffs – neglected in summer – produce a clutch of popular ice-falls after periods of severe frost.

**Approaches:** All routes described in this section can be approached from the A5 trunk road, which passes down the length of the Ogwen Valley between Glyders and Carneddau. There is no regular public transport between Capel Curig and Bethesda (infrequent bus service in summer).

**Accommodation:** *Camping*: Dol-gam, 3km east of Capel Curig near A5 (GR.746 574); Gwern Gof Isaf, 5km west of Capel Curig near A5 (GR.685 602); Gwern Gof Uchaf, 6km north-west of Capel Curig near A5 (GR.673 604); Garth Farm, 2km south-west of Capel Curig near A4086 (GR.702 571).
*High camps/bivouacs*: Cwm Eigiau (for Craig yr Ysfa); Cwm Llafar (for Llech Ddu); Cwm Bochlwyd (for Glyder Fach).
*Bunkhouses/barns:* Gwern Gof Isaf, 5km north-west of Capel Curig near A5 (GR.685 602). Several climbing clubs have huts in the valley.
*Youth Hostels*: Capel Curig and Idwal Cottage.
*Hotels/B&B*: Hotels plus numerous Bed and Breakfast houses in Capel Curig and Bethesda.

**Services:** Capel Curig has several pubs and cafés, a post office-cum-general store, two equipment shops, public toilets, telephone, and a petrol station (1km east of the village centre). Bethesda, a small town, has all the above plus garage services, mini-markets, take-away food and drink, and so on. At Ogwen Cottage there are toilets, a telephone, and a kiosk.

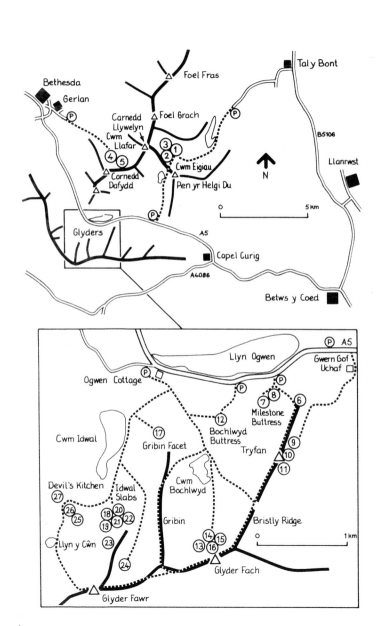

*The Narrows of Soapgut (Route 8), Milestone Buttress. The stance is optional.*

Below the overhang on Lot's Groove (Route 16), Glyder Fach.
The Chasm is to its right, and the upper cracks of Lot's Wife to its
left. The climbers top left are on the crucial final crack of Direct
Route.

# 1: AMPHITHEATRE BUTTRESS (VD) 300m

**Summary:** A satisfying expedition in remote surroundings. Most difficulties arise in the lower part, culminating in the exposed barrier pitch.

**First Ascent:** G. D. Abraham, A. P. Abraham, D. Leighton and J. W. Puttrell, May 1905.

**Best Conditions:** Dries quickly after rain in summer, despite a northerly aspect and 600m altitude. Unpleasant and difficult when wet. Start early to beat queues and catch the sun!

**Approach:** (1) From Tal y Bont in the Conwy Valley. A single track road leaves the B5106 at GR.767 688, rising steeply westwards. Follow it for about 5km to its terminus in Cwm Eigiau (refer to Ogwen Area map). Parking for several cars (avoid obstructing gate). Continue along the rough track for 5km, passing Llyn Eigiau, to old quarry buildings. Cross marshland to the crag at GR.694 637. 1hr 30 mins.
(2) From Ogwen as for Route 3.

**Starting Point:** A scree-filled couloir issues from the central Amphitheatre. Start at the slabby foot of the narrow buttress to its left.

**Descent:** Turn right to ascend Carnedd Llywelyn, or descend left (some scrambling) to the Ogwen approach col and regain the start by this route.

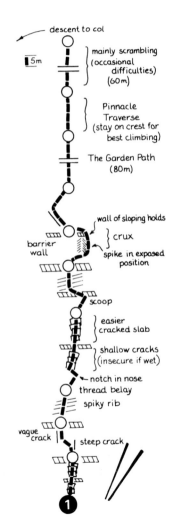

descent to col

5m

mainly scrambling (occasional difficulties) (60m)

Pinnacle Traverse (stay on crest for best climbing)

The Garden Path (80m)

wall of sloping holds

crux

barrier wall

spike in exposed position

scoop

easier cracked slab

shallow cracks (insecure if wet)

notch in nose
thread belay

spiky rib

vague crack

steep crack

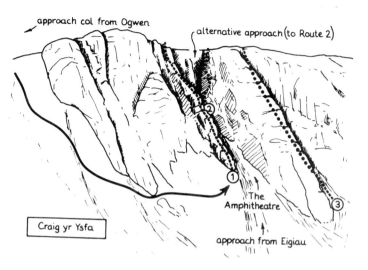

approach col from Ogwen

alternative approach (to Route 2)

The Amphitheatre

approach from Eigiau

Craig yr Ysfa

The Ogwen approach to Craig yr Ysfa is unkind on feet and morale. A midday toil up the slope from Ffynnon Llugwy to the col severely tests enthusiasm. Aesthetes and alpinists instead approach at dawn from Cwm Eigiau, carrying little equipment but many sandwiches for the long day ahead.

In high summer the inviting lower slabs bake in the morning sun, appetisers for the typical fare of an Ogwen buttress which follows: spiky ribs, polished cracks, blocks, scoops and noses – all mixed together and liberally garnished with heather.

The *mauvais quart d'heure* arrives at half height. Here the dry-mouthed second gulps while his leader, sickened by an awesome drop into the Amphitheatre, works up the edge. But the barrier is short, its holds large, and protection never far away.

The *Garden Path* soothes nerves in readiness for the *Pinnacle Traverse* – scenic high point of the route. Here the alpinists come into their own, moving together at great speed towards the top where they will pause only to coil the rope and eat sandwiches, before steaming off towards Carnedd Llywelyn. The overtaken will nurse dented pride and wish blisters on them.

# 2: MUR Y NIWL/PINNACLE WALL (VS+) 150m

**Summary:** An impressive and improbable climb up the vertical Amphitheatre Wall. Complex route finding and unremitting exposure provide situations as serious as any in Wales. Sound rock and adequate protection on the crucial passages. Double ropes strongly recommended.

**First Ascent:** Mur y Niwl – A. J. J. Moulam and J. B. Churchill, April 1952. Pinnacle Wall – C. F. Kirkus, June 1931.

**Best Conditions:** Although the crag is at 600m, the Amphitheatre Wall faces south-east and catches the summer sun. The walls dry within a day or two of rain, but the cracks may carry drainage for some time.

**Approach:** (1) From the Ogwen Valley. Approach as for Route 3 to the col, but then turn left and ascend the ridge to emerge above the crag at GR.692 637. Leave rucksacks here and descend the right side (looking in) of the shallow Amphitheatre Gully – very steep with occasional down-climbing sections – to gain the foot of the Lower Amphitheatre Wall. Refer to Ogwen Area map and Route 1 diagram. 2 hrs.

(2) From the Conwy Valley as for Route 1.

**Starting Point:** Below the bottom step in the gully, where a 6m wall leads up to the left end of a narrow, grass ledge.

**Descent:** Descend the ridge leftwards to regain the approach col.

In 1932 Colin Kirkus struggled up The Crack, a vicious problem up the left side of the Lower Amphitheatre Wall, but failed to solve the main challenge of the central wall. Its exposed situations and bold hand traverses, and the uncertain prospect of downward escape, had unnerved even this most determined of climbers. The ascent twenty years later of Mur y Niwl – The Wall of Mists – was a milestone in Carneddau climbing and in the career of Tony Moulam. Although several good climbs have since breached the wall, including a fascinating *E2* girdle traverse, none can match the elegance and cunning of the original.

Kirkus had already claimed the best line on the Upper Wall. Climbing solo, he circumvented the blank lower section by traversing The Quartz Pavement – a unique sloping gangway. Like many who follow, he must have hesitated at a committing stride across the gap at its end. He resolved to go on, his boldness rewarded by a satisfying escape up secure cracks.

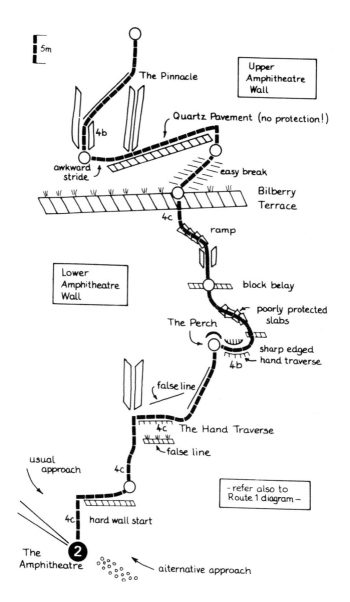

5m

The Pinnacle

Upper Amphitheatre Wall

Quartz Pavement (no protection!)

4b

awkward stride

easy break

Bilberry Terrace

4c

ramp

Lower Amphitheatre Wall

block belay

poorly protected slabs

The Perch

sharp edged hand traverse

4b

false line

The Hand Traverse

4c

false line

usual approach

4c

refer also to Route 1 diagram

4c

hard wall start

The Amphitheatre

2

alternative approach

# 3: GREAT GULLY (S or IV) 250m

**Summary:** A classic gully climb having an oppressive atmosphere, two notorious obstacles, and the usual quota of vegetable matter. The deep snow of a good winter obscures some vegetation but few pitches.

**First Ascent:** J. M. A. Thomson, R. I. Simey and W. G. Clay, April 1900.

**Best Conditions:** Rarely dry throughout, although a relative lack of drainage allows the Converging Walls and the Great Cave Pitch to dry out in summer within a few days of rain, despite a northerly aspect and 600m altitude. Conversely this restricts ice accumulation in winter, when deep, consolidated snow will give the best chance of success.

**Approach:** (1) From the Ogwen Valley. Park at a lay-by on the A5 at GR.688 603, 400m west of Helyg (limited space – do not obstruct the gate), and ascend the Electricity Board access road towards Ffynnon Llugwy. Leave the road where it veers towards the lake, and continue by a path which rises to the col between the summit of Craig yr Ysfa on the left (the crag itself lies hidden on the far side of the ridge) and Pen yr Helgi Du on the right. Descend heather slopes on the far side of the col, at first contouring left (looking out) and then descending diagonally left by scree runnels and zigzag troughs to the foot of the left-hand section of the crag. (For Route 1, ascend rightwards to gain the foot of the

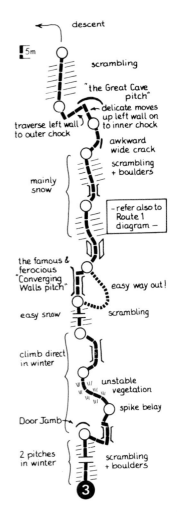

descent

5m

scrambling

"the Great Cave pitch"

delicate moves up left wall on to inner chock

traverse left wall to outer chock

awkward wide crack

scrambling + boulders

mainly snow

– refer also to Route 1 diagram –

the famous & ferocious "Converging Walls pitch"

easy way out!

easy snow

scrambling

climb direct in winter

unstable vegetation

spike belay

Door Jamb

2 pitches in winter

scrambling + boulders

③

buttress.) Cross the central scree cone below the Amphitheatre and pass below the right-hand section of the crag. Ascend on grass to the gully entrance. During this approach the gully remains hidden throughout; avoid entering the false line of Vanishing Gully (which does) just right of the lowest point of the buttress. Refer to Ogwen Area map and Route 1 diagram. GR.694 638. 1hr 45mins. (In deep powder snow this approach may take up to 4hrs.)

(2) From the Conwy Valley as for Route 1 (road to Cwm Eigiau sometimes impassable in winter).

**Starting Point:** Summer – below the first dripping chockstone. Winter – below and right of the gully entrance.

**Descent:** Descend the ridge leftwards to regain the approach col.

Most gullies are horrible, some are tolerable, a few are good, and just a handful – this one among them – are great. Its reputation rests on the inescapable Great Cave pitch, which alone separates beleaguered climbers from the easy runnel leading to the top. But the true connoisseur, being someone who – perhaps unwisely – has climbed the route both summer and winter, knows that the real watershed will be crossed earlier in the day at the Converging Walls pitch. Here only the skilful and resolute are destined to succeed (the remainder will scuttle up an easy variant on the right!).

One of the converging walls drips with green slime, the other overhangs. In summer you face west and stuff a crack in the leaning wall full of runners and fingers; in winter you face east and back-and-foot your crampons up the frozen slime.

The Great Cave is a fearful place. What if damp or verglas thwarts your traverse of its left wall? Unlike some chockstone pitches this one will not respond to combined tactics or other subterfuge and the prospect of retreat is not pleasant. In winter, darkness threatens to confine you – as so many climbers before – to a shivering vigil in the Cave. If you listen carefully, before settling down to bivouac, you may hear whoops of joy from those having narrowly escaped the night. Try to forgive.

# 4: THE GROOVE (E1) 135m

**Summary:** A tremendous climb on a remote mountain crag – one of the great Welsh *Extremes*. A powerful atmosphere swamps comparatively modest technicalities.

**First Ascent:** J. V. Anthoine and I. F. Campbell, October 1961.

**Best Conditions:** The crag faces north at an altitude of 600m. Its lichenous rock requires several fine summer days to dry out after rain.

**Approach:** Turn right at crossroads just south of Bethesda (when approaching from Ogwen). Turn right after 1km at a second set of crossroads, and find a parking space, taking care not to obstruct gates or passing places. Walk towards the road end. Cross a stile right of the waterworks gate, and another at the top left corner of the field. Beyond a third stile, follow the stream bed through its culvert, and then a drier path to open ground. Enter Cwm Llafar on a good track to arrive at huge boulders below the crag at GR.666 637. Refer to Ogwen Area map. 1hr.

**Starting Point:** At a slim groove below a sickly tree on the grass terrace at 25m.

**Descent:** Traverse right and descend short walls and grass ledges (move further right if in doubt).

Llech Ddu ranks alongside Cyrn Las in the league of heavyweights and yet fails to attract a regular clientele. This sombre spur of Carnedd Dafydd has never been fashionable. Few climbers realise their ambition to ascend The Groove, and of those who do hardly any want to repeat the experience. It's that kind of climb.

An obstinate little groove is mere preamble. Above, a leering fissure substitutes for the main groove which fails to reach the terrace. It is slimy, difficult, and not well protected. Safely coaxed up the crux, the second now pioneers left on finger flakes while the leader crouches on his inadequate perch and struggles to suppress a growing anxiety.

The new leader has found The Groove, but not much of a stance from which to belay its ascent. Now both climbers are terrified. They try to comfort each other but the shiver in their voices only makes things worse. Beneath them stretches lonely Cwm Llafar, empty and echoing. Tension evaporates with the momentous discovery that The Groove responds to ordinary effort: bridging, jamming, lay-aways. Hard but honest.

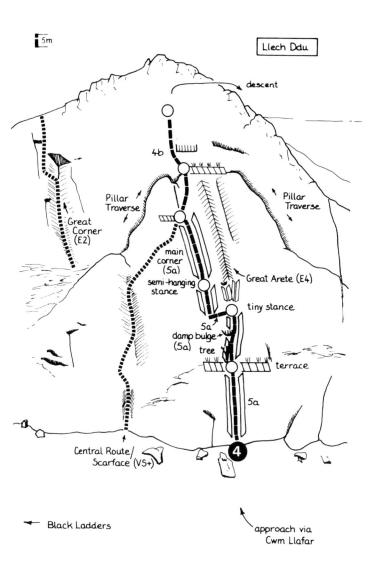

# 5: WESTERN GULLY (IV) 300m

**Summary:** A remote gully which fully deserves its fearsome reputation. Protection and belays usually good, although the crucial slab pitch – scene of many failures – is difficult to protect when thinly iced.

**First Ascent:** Winter – probably J. Brown and R. Moseley, 1952.

**Best Conditions:** North facing at high altitude and therefore frequently in good condition; but vulnerable to sudden thawing from coastal air. Character and difficulty of the route vary tremendously according to build-up.

**Approach:** From Bethesda. Approach initially as for Route 4, continuing to the head of the cwm (refer to Ogwen Area map). Few lines penetrate the lower rock barrier, and consequently in cloud it is almost impossible to locate their starts. GR.670 632. 1hr 45mins (but allow 2hrs or more in deep snow).

**Starting Point:** Refer to crag diagram. In good conditions the lower barrier may be climbed direct on difficult ice; otherwise zigzag up snow patches on the left, and traverse a snow ramp to the foot of the gully proper.

**Descent:** Circle left to a shallow col at GR.683 637. Descend left (northwest) into Cwm Llafar and regain the approach path.

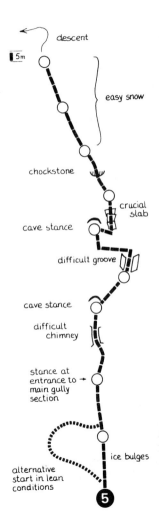

descent

5m

easy snow

chockstone

crucial slab

cave stance

difficult groove

cave stance

difficult chimney

stance at entrance to → main gully section

ice bulges

alternative start in lean conditions

**5**

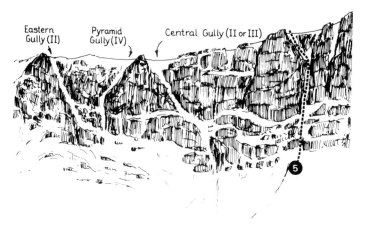

Black Ladders

Eastern Gully (II)   Pyramid Gully (IV)   Central Gully (II or III)

**5**

In summer, the Black Ladders perpetually ooze drainage water from a porous skin. In a good winter, these seepages defy a coastal influence and freeze into a fretwork of discontinuous ice flows. These become the hard direct starts and finishes to a collection of otherwise uninspiring snow gullies. Western Gully also suffers a major discontinuity near its base, but then fully asserts itself as the major line on the cliff.

The gully is so sensitive to conditions that some climbers have waited a decade to make the ascent (some wait still), while others saunter up Cwm Llafar during their first season, encounter copious quantities of ice, and romp up the route in a couple of hours.

The rock is reasonably accommodating if you can get at it. But if those conditions prevail then there will be insufficient ice for front-pointing and you will be consigned to thrutching up impending grooves while crampons scrattle and axes dangle. The slab exit from the cave settles the outcome. Straightforward under those rare conditions of thick ice, it poses a tricky rock problem when bare. When covered with verglas it frustrates all attempts, and sentences the hapless few to yet another decade of waiting.

# 6: NORTHERN RIDGES (E or I/II) 8km

**Summary:** A magnificent horseshoe traverse high above Cwm Bochlwyd, and including the summits of Tryfan and Glyder Fach. In summer, an easy scrambling expedition of sustained interest (grade applies to optional, direct variants). Under snow, it becomes a much more serious outing, comparable then to a winter traverse of the Snowdon Horseshoe (Route 47). Axes, crampons and rope are essential in these conditions.

**Best Conditions:** Good conditions for a winter traverse are rare, an insidious mixture of powder snow and hoar-frost being typical. Best avoided when verglased or when deep powder obscures the ledges. Poor visibility can lead to route finding errors while crossing the summit plateau of Glyder Fach.

**Starting Point:** At the Milestone lay-by (GR.663 603) on the A5 in the Ogwen Valley.

**Emergency Descents:** From Bwlch Tryfan into Cwm Bochlwyd. In difficult winter conditions, of ice or deep powder, consider escaping Glyder Fach by descending east (avoiding a false line which leads into the couloir on the east side of Bristly Ridge) to Llyn Caseg Fraith, finally descending the ridge northwards to Gwern Gof Isaf.

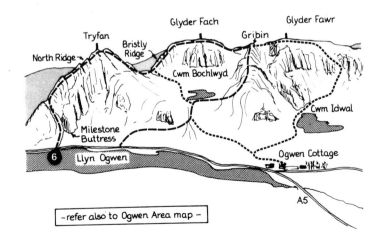

Tryfan casts down its North Ridge in a single sweep towards the valley. A heather and scree shoulder at one-third height is the first objective, laboriously gained using a boulder-covered rake which slants up from below the Milestone Buttress.

Above the shoulder, the ridge begins to assert itself (look out for the Cannon on the right) and eventually narrows to a rock rib. Taken direct this presents the first scrambling challenge. In winter, a left-flanking path avoids this insecure step. Either route leads to a notch and short scramble to the North Summit. Simple boulder hopping gains the Central summit.

A direct descent of the South Ridge to Bwlch Tryfan presents few difficulties summer or winter, although in bad visibility it is easy to stray from its broad back. A more serious worry in these conditions is in finding the start of Bristly Ridge. The most reliable strategy is to follow the stone wall up to the first crags, and then traverse ten metres right to enter a small gully. Move left at its top, over a constructed wall, to access the main gully. With minor deviations this leads on to the main part of the ridge. In winter, a more reliable gully approach can be found further left.

Route finding up the remainder of the ridge is less complicated. Entry and exit at the Great Pinnacle Gap pose the main problems, although even these are slight unless conditions are very bad. The ridge beyond finally merges into the boulder-covered summit plateau of Glyder Fach.

The route between Glyder Fach summit and the top of the Gribin contains few technical difficulties but many opportunities for getting lost. In bad visibility a popular but unnecessary southern detour avoids the rock pile of Castell y Gwynt. From a shallow col beyond, locate the Gribin in mist by ignoring the main path to Glyder Fawr and staying close to the lip above Cwm Bochlwyd.

Only the top section of the Gribin presents any difficulty. The easiest route zigzags down short steps on its west flank until a path leads over scree to a grass shoulder. Under powder snow this descent demands special care, since many of the smaller spikes and traverse ledges will be obscured. The remainder of the ridge dips more gently towards Ogwen – idyllic in the evening sunshine.

# 7: DIRECT ROUTE (VD) 90m

**Summary:** An Ogwen classic, polished by decades of struggle. Includes both strenuous and delicate climbing. Spacious stances and adequate protection.

**First Ascent:** G. Barlow and H. Priestly-Smith, August 1910.

**Best Conditions:** West facing at 400m. Little vegetation remains; on a breezy summer day the route can dry within hours of rain (except for a drainage streak in the top chimney). Unpleasant and insecure when wet. Catches the afternoon sun from spring through to autumn.

**Approach:** From the Milestone lay-by on the A5 (GR.663 603). Ascend near a stone wall, cross it at a ladder stile, and contour rightwards to gain the lowest point of the cliff. Ascend right then left, bypassing the first little step, to arrive below the slabby west face at GR.663 601. Refer to Ogwen area map. 20mins.

**Starting Point:** A blunt rib defines the left side of the face. Start below an obvious diagonal crack which splits the wrinkled slab to its right.

**Descent:** This demands care. Traverse right across a small gully to easy angled slabs. Cross these rightwards, descending slightly, and enter the gully on the right side of the crag. Cross to its far side and descend over scree and short steps.

Few climbs of this standard can boast such absorbing technicality. Interest begins at once with some carefully judged friction moves up the diagonal crack, boot rubber squeaking in its polished scoops. At the slab apex the timid will disappear inside a crevasse, perhaps forever, while the bold reach left to a comfortable flake and swing into a hand traverse.

A crack above the pinnacle belay springs a knee vice on the unwary, but otherwise the pitch culminates in an exposed crossing beneath a leaning block. There's talk of hand traverses here, but precise footwork and good runners will render it harmless.

The dreaded chimney arrives. A fickle thing, it resists entry until violated and then positively sucks you inside. Progress is made facing right, the exit facing left. Typically perverse.

A dozen variants await those who have tired of the normal route. The left-hand start, which includes a juggy overhang, is particularly exciting at no increase in standard. *VS* pitches up the rib to its left provide the Superdirect with its Bastard Layback (which is), and a beautiful jamming crack.

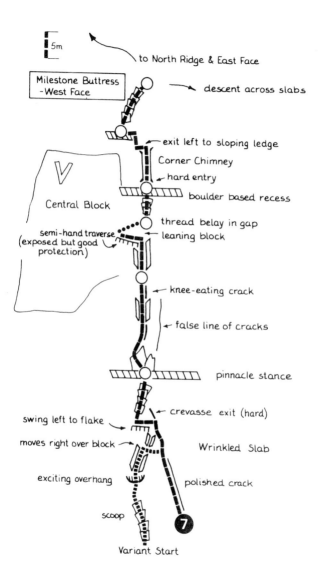

5m

to North Ridge & East Face

Milestone Buttress
– West Face

descent across slabs

exit left to sloping ledge

Corner Chimney

hard entry

boulder based recess

Central Block

thread belay in gap

leaning block

semi-hand traverse
(exposed but good
protection)

knee-eating crack

false line of cracks

pinnacle stance

crevasse exit (hard)

swing left to flake

moves right over block

Wrinkled Slab

exciting overhang

polished crack

scoop

7

Variant Start

# 8: SOAPGUT/CHIMNEY ROUTE (VS) 60m

**Summary:** A pleasant corner and wicked chimney combine to give a disjointed climb up the sunless Back Wall of the Milestone. The gut is conventional and well protected, the chimney is not.

**First Ascent:** Soapgut – J. M. Edwards and C. W. F. Noyce, September 1936. Chimney Route – E. W. Steeple and G. Barlow, August 1913.

**Best Conditions:** North facing at 400m. Rain run-off, which once irrigated a vegetable patch in the gut, today sluices unhindered down a clean corner. Consequently, in summer the route will dry in three days or less (though in winter hardly ever). Chimney Route is not to be contemplated when wet.

**Approach:** As for Route 7, but instead of crossing the stile continue up the left side of the wall. 15mins.

**Starting Point:** Directly below the prominent corner which is a distinctive feature of the face.

**Descent:** As for Route 7.

Soapgut continues to enjoy something of a reputation among Ogwen *habitués*. It must be during one's impressionable years, while labouring up the Milestone path *en route* for the gentler West Face, that it implants the seed of desire.

Although the corner begins without complication its supply of holds evaporates in inverse proportion to the water which trickles down its angle. This leaves one high and dry, so to speak, an arm's length short of the half-way ledge. Beyond it a slender ramp regains the corner at the Narrows, where polished nicks betray a long history of nervous bridging. Nowadays, a secure runner and friction footwear ease the pain of a finger-jamming exit.

The true line of the gut continues directly, while the Chimney finish lurks beyond the right-hand rib. The leader will catch a glimpse of it while anchoring to the *gendarme* which directs traffic hereabouts. It is not a pretty sight.

Warning bells start to ring at an opening bout of friction bridging. A lurch up to the right brings momentary relief in a wide crack. Unfortunately the move is irreversible and the crack has no more holds. But to panic is to die. Instead udge up a couple of moves and slot a runner in the corner on the left. This clears the mind wonderfully, so much so that all sorts of holds suddenly begin to materialise. The rest is easy.

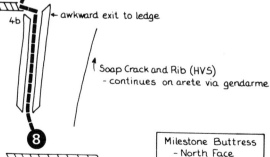

descent across slabs

5m

original finish of Soap Gut

gendarme
stance

Central Block

evil chimney/crack
4b

4b

The Narrows

original start
of Chimney Route

possible
stance

4b ← delicate step across to ramp

4b ← awkward exit to ledge

↑ Soap Crack and Rib (HVS)
– continues on arete via gendarme

⑧

Milestone Buttress
– North Face

terrace below prominent corner

# 9: GROOVED ARÊTE (VD+) 240m

**Summary:** A famous mountaineering route of great character – the best on Tryfan. Polished rock adds delicacy to crucial passages.

**First Ascent:** E. W. Steeple, A. G. Woodhouse, G. Barlow, H. E. Brown and A. H. Doughty, April 1911.

**Best Conditions:** Faces east at high altitude, but in summer will dry within a day or two of rain.

**Approach:** From Gwern Gof Uchaf (GR.673 604). Follow the path south-west, passing below the huge slab of Little Tryfan (excellent three-pitch route of *M* standard up its left edge). Ascend a badly eroded gully to the indistinct beginnings of Heather Terrace (refer to Ogwen area map). Monitor progress along the terrace by identifying gullies: Bastow lies deep within rock walls; Nor'Nor' resembles Bastow and is scree-filled at its base; Green has a grassy bed and defines the right side of North Buttress. GR.666 595. 1hr.

**Starting Point:** 6m left of Green Gully, below a small corner.

**Descent:** Descend the North Ridge to a scree and heather shoulder. Contour east to the top of the eroded approach gully. Alternatively, ascend leftwards to the Central Summit and descend as for Route 10 or 11.

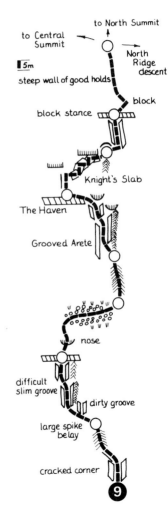

to North Summit

to Central Summit

North Ridge descent

5m

steep wall of good holds

block

block stance

block

Knight's Slab

The Haven

Grooved Arête

nose

difficult slim groove

dirty groove

large spike belay

cracked corner

**9**

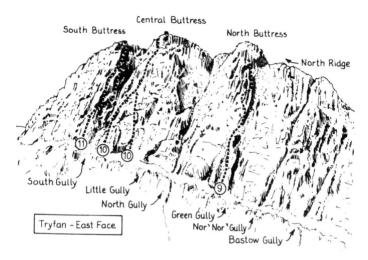

South Buttress • Central Buttress • North Buttress • North Ridge

(11) (10) (10)

South Gully • Little Gully • North Gully • Green Gully • Nor'Nor'Gully • Bastow Gully • (9)

Tryfan - East Face

Tryfan's East Face straddles the boundary between scrambling and rock climbing. The proximity of heather runnels can make it all seem rather pointless. Fortunately on Grooved Arête the side walls of groove pitches make efficient blinkers! Technically these polished chutes are as difficult as anything above. Beyond the top groove a gentle stroll helps work up an appetite for lunch.

The buttress now gathers itself into an imposing tower, throwing down the gauntlet of the grooved arête itself. Challenge or lure? Victors gather at the Haven and speculate on their future. Clouds invariably choose this moment to swirl down from the summit ridge, enveloping the face in a moist wrap. The Knight's Slab is above.

Knight's moves guide the leader diagonally across the chess-board to a notch in its right skyline. Perched on this tiny stance, he prays his clumsy second will not slither screaming from his holds to fetch up somewhere inaccessible, groaning and immobile. Although dark grooves and unknown difficulties lie ahead, he knows this is the psychological turning point. Gathering up rope he shouts encouragement to his companion, but he knows the outcome is in other hands. Adventure must run its course.

# 10: PINNACLE RIB (VD+) 175m

**Summary:** A typical East Face mountaineering route – friendly but mischievous. Expect delays at the Yellow Slab while Ogwen novices are ritually blooded.

**First Ascent:** First Pinnacle Rib – E. W. Steeple, G. Barlow and A. H. Doughty, September 1914; Second Pinnacle Rib – J. M. A. Thomson and H. Hughes, October 1894.

**Best Conditions:** Despite its high altitude, it should dry within a day or two of rain (except Thomson's Chimney, which pleases itself).

**Approach:** Initially as for Route 9. Continue along Heather Terrace to the heather bay at the foot of Central Buttress. GR.665 594. 1hr 15mins.

**Starting Point:** There are two approaches to the Yellow Slab; refer to diagram for location.

**Descent:** Follow a path down to the amphitheatre above North Gully. Either cross it to descend as for Route 9, or descend the easy upper part of the gully to follow a narrow path across the wall on the right (looking out). This enters the subsidiary Little Gully which, with some scrambling, eventually emerges on Heather Terrace between North Gully and the heather bay. Alternatively, descend from the summit as for Route 11.

First Pinnacle Rib begins promisingly with an overhung slab and grooved rib. The nondescript but pleasant ridge which follows is typical of the face. Before long it degenerates into broken steps leading to the huge Pinnacle. Second Pinnacle Rib, part of the route pioneered by Archer Thomson, offers more continuous climbing in its approach to the Pinnacle.

Preliminaries over, the Yellow Slab takes centre stage. Evidence of skittering boot soles is all around, but the best hope of success lies immediately behind the Pinnacle. By using ripples on the slab's left edge you should be able to adhere long enough to pull into a slim groove, which thankfully soon eases. None of this is too serious but, if all else fails, there is an easier alternative to the right.

A curled leaf of rock maintains interest for one more pitch, but beyond that the route loses integrity. Those looking for a bit more excitement will find it in Thomson's Chimney – a nasty piece of work on the Final Wall. The Chimney is obvious, and is gained from a ledge and crack up the left side of the block which obstructs it. The upper crack presents the greatest difficulty: enter if you can; continue if you must.

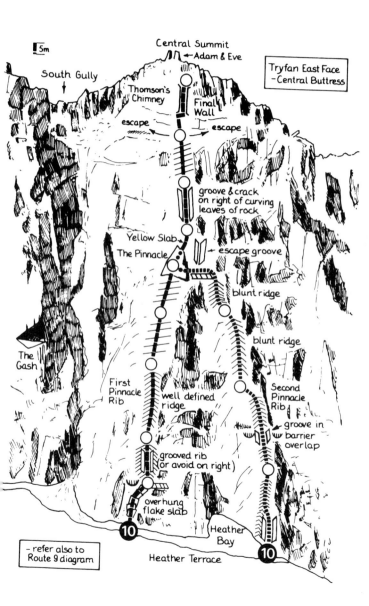

Tryfan East Face
–Central Buttress

Central Summit
← Adam & Eve

South Gully

Thomson's Chimney

Final Wall

escape → ← escape

groove & crack on right of curving leaves of rock

Yellow Slab

The Pinnacle ← escape groove

blunt ridge

blunt ridge

The Gash

First Pinnacle Rib

well defined ridge

Second Pinnacle Rib

groove in barrier overlap

grooved rib (or avoid on right)

overhung flake slab

⑩

Heather Bay

⑩

– refer also to Route 9 diagram

Heather Terrace

5m

# 11: GASHED CRAG (VD+) & MUNICH (VS) 210m

**Summary:** A fine mountaineering route with optional *VS* climbing for technocrats. Less heather and more rock than usual for this face. Chimney cracks instil terror, but build character.

**First Ascent:** Gashed Crag – H. B. Buckle and G. Barlow, September 1902. Munich – H. Teufel, H. Sedlmayr and J. R. Jenkins, July 1936.

**Best Conditions:** Carries no more drainage than other East Face routes but the chimney cracks (and the Munich slab) see less of the sun, which doesn't help at this high altitude. These pitches are not nice when wet. Allow a couple of good drying days after bad weather.

**Approach:** Via Heather Terrace as for Route 10 to South Gully. Continue along the terrace for a short distance to the top of a steep rise in the path. GR.665 593. 1hr 15mins.

**Starting Point:** About 20m left of South Gully, at a groove below an overhang.

**Descent:** Descend the South Ridge to a pronounced col. Descend a shallow couloir on the east side until vague paths lead left (looking out) on to the indistinct upper part of Heather Terrace. Note how easy it is to descend too far and miss the terrace altogether! Alternatively, ascend rightwards to the Central Summit and descend as for Route 9 or 10.

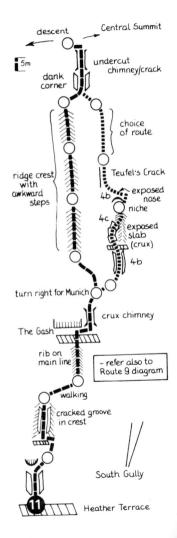

Memories of climbing the East Face are compiled from jumbled recollections of jug-pulling orgies up the sunny side of ridges, of sleepy interludes on bilberry ledges, and of intoxicated pirouettes on the summit stones after making the symbolic leap from Adam to Eve. Tryfan is the mother of mountaineers.

Gashed Crag contributes to this idyll – up to a point. It begins like all the others, with a groove and a ridge and a walk, but then deliberately seeks out uncertainty at the Gash, which a little chimney crack on the right promises to resolve. There are scratches on holds so deep inside this crack that one wonders what could possibly have made them (or indeed if it still lurks within). Humanoids must resort to wedging up the crack with the left leg while ineffectually pumping the right foot up the outside slab. The technique resembles kick-starting an old motor bike, though for all the good it does you may as well be flogging a dead horse (which if you think about it amounts to the same thing). Surprisingly, after five metres of this, the brutalised chimney gives up.

As an expert who demolished the previous pitch ('What pitch?') you now have an opportunity to show off by finishing up Munich. First, get yourself across to a slim groove, and climb it to the base of an obvious, rectangular slab. Ascend this by trending rightwards to an exposed finish, up the right edge. Escape the constricted stance by somehow gaining the nose above, and traversing it leftwards into the security of Teufel's Crack. But we were on Gashed Crag, above the chimney . . .

A steepening wall continues its sinister theme, but then an unlikely series of holds leads left to rediscover the ridge's friendlier flank. It nevertheless chooses to be awkward on several occasions during the two or three pitches remaining, before the final wall arrives.

Over on the right, a dank corner leads to an undercut crack and memory flashbacks of earlier struggles. Luckily this one eases almost at once. It lands you quite suddenly on the South Summit, where seagulls await your sandwiches. They must have seen you coming.

# 12: BOCHLWYD MAIN FACE (VD+, S+ or HVS) 40m

**Summary:** A trio of varied outcrop climbs on a compact buttress within easy reach of Ogwen. Universally steep but on good rock.

**First Ascent:** Chimney Climb – F. Aldous, A. C. Adams and O. Thorneycroft, August 1909. Wall Climb – F. E. Hicks, C. V. A. Cooper and W. E. Woosnam Jones, September 1929. Bochlwyd Eliminate – R. James and R. Barber, June 1962.

**Best Conditions:** North-west facing at 400m but carries little drainage; at best will dry within hours of rain. An ideal venue for summer evenings, when it catches the setting sun.

**Approach:** (1) From a car-park on the A5 at GR.659 602, 1km east of Ogwen Cottage. Ascend a boulder slope on the west side of the car-park then trend rightwards over boggy ground to reach the crag.

(2) From Ogwen Cottage via the initial section of the Bochlwyd path, contouring left to reach the foot of the crag at GR.657 597. Refer to Ogwen Area map. 20mins by either route.

**Starting Point:** All three routes start in the vicinity of the prominent central chimney line.

**Descent:** Down the shallow couloir which defines the right side of the buttress.

Bochlwyd's shapely profile distracts climbers from their central purpose, which is a big climb on Glyder Fach. A profusion of incut holds more than compensates for the high angle – a half-hour diversion has a habit of becoming a half-day preoccupation.

Chimney Climb (*VD+*) ignores a direct entry and begins energetically up a rib near its right-hand branch. An overhang protects the upper chimney, but by squirming up towards it you will find a good hold by which to effect an entry.

Wall Climb (*S+*) takes a more devious line. It begins up a ramp which rises below the smoothest wall on the crag, but then steps down and left to struggle up an overhanging crack. The top pitch up the exposed left edge of the main wall is pure delight.

Bochlwyd Eliminate (*HVS*) also begins up the Wall Climb gangway (or reaches it direct), but then accepts the main challenge of the buttress. A step up from the gangway reveals a previously hidden traverse leading into the centre of the face. From here a lucky sequence of finger flakes zigzags up the wall, producing a lonely but satisfying lead.

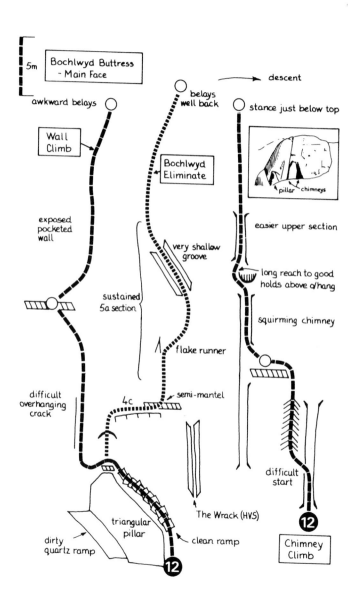

5m

Bochlwyd Buttress
– Main Face

→ descent

awkward belays

Wall Climb

belays well back

stance just below top

Bochlwyd Eliminate

exposed pocketed wall

easier upper section

very shallow groove

long reach to good holds above o/hang

sustained 5a section

squirming chimney

flake runner

difficult overhanging crack

4c

semi-mantel

pillar  chimneys

The Wrack (HVS)

difficult start

dirty quartz ramp

triangular pillar

clean ramp

12

12

Chimney Climb

# 13: CENTRAL GULLY (II/III) 300m

**Summary:** A traditional gully climb of about eight pitches, including an awkward ice entry, a straightforward middle section on snow, and a scenic finish over mixed ground. Beautifully situated high above Cwm Bochlwyd.

**First Ascent:** Winter – not known.

**Best Conditions:** North-west facing at an altitude above 800m. The gully carries comparatively little drainage and so reaches optimum condition under deep, consolidated snow. Good ice accumulation allows a direct ascent of the entry pitches. Adequate belays can usually be found among flanking rocks.

**Approach:** From Ogwen Cottage car-park (GR.649 604) on the A5 between Capel Curig and Bethesda (overspill parking near by). Follow the main Idwal path for a few minutes to where it bends right. Now bear left, over grass then stepping-stones, to ascend the badly eroded path right of the stream which issues from Cwm Bochlwyd. Circle Llyn Bochlwyd on its left, and ascend boulder slopes to below the right side of the cliff. Refer to Ogwen Area map. GR.654 584. 1hr, in good conditions.

**Starting Point:** At the shallow gully entrance (refer to crag drawing). Note that, despite its name, the gully is not at all central to the cliffs. For this reason, attempts have been made in the past to rename it West Gully, but common usage prevails here.

**Descent:** The route leads naturally on to the summit of Glyder Fach itself. Route finding on the summit plateau in bad visibility can be extremely difficult. In daylight, and under suitable conditions, the Gribin Ridge ((Route 6) makes a convenient descent. Alternatively, retrace Route 6 as far as the emergence of Bristly Ridge, and descend the couloir on its east side to Bwlch Tryfan (GR.662 588). Descend north-west from this col into Cwm Bochlwyd. If the couloir does not appeal then consider descending to Gwern Gof Isaf via Llyn Caseg Fraith as noted under *Emergency Descents* for Route 6.

The gullies of Glyder Fach ought to give interesting winter climbs. Unfortunately they carry less drainage than appearances suggest, and the snow conditions required to bring out the best in them rarely materialise. Consequently most routes retain much of their summer character, including struggles with chimneys and chockstones. Central Gully is the exception, as it maintains a winter identity throughout its length.

The route can be divided into three stages: ice entry, snow

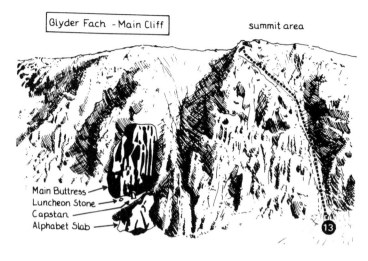

Glyder Fach - Main Cliff

summit area

Main Buttress
Luncheon Stone
Capstan
Alphabet Slab

13

interlude, and mixed finish. The entry poses the greatest problems. Depending on conditions its ascent may involve delicate work over thinly iced slabs, grooves and chimneys. Fortunately the gully here is more of a broad recess, offering many opportunities for turning difficulties.

At a little over a third of the way up the cliff reclines and the route assumes the character of a conventional snow gully. The bed remains broad but well defined in its impressive sweep up to the left. In a good year there are several possibilities for direct finishes; otherwise the main gully will be followed in its entirety to a small col.

The col is in fact a notch in the shallow ridge which, in its lower reaches, bounds the left side of the gully. In bad visibility this will cause great confusion – particularly if the mists part to reveal the distinctive bulk of Tryfan ahead, which intuitively you feel ought to be behind! The final section of the route, therefore, lies up to the right on the bouldery back of this ridge – awkward at first, but easing as it rises towards the twisted, hoar frosted sculptures of the summit plateau.

# 14: CHASM ROUTE (VD+) 80m

**Summary:** A unique climb up the rift bounding the right side of Glyder Fach's main buttress. A grass break at half height barely detracts from its rugged character. Miscalculations at the Vice will result in a desperate struggle (troglodytes may prefer the alternative Subterranean Exit).

**First Ascent:** J. M. A. Thomson, H. O. Jones and L. Noon, Easter 1910.

**Best Conditions:** North-west facing at 800m. Water seeps from corner cracks in the lower chasm at most times, although this affects the outcome less than might be expected. The Vice must be dry, which is often the case after a couple of fine summer days.

**Approach:** As for Route 13. Ascend scree and broken rocks on the left side of the Alphabet Slabs to a level area at their apex. Refer to Route 13 crag diagram. GR.656 585. 1hr.

**Starting Point:** At the foot of a vegetated gully leading into the Chasm.

**Descent:** (1) Continue to the summit and descend as for Route 13.
(2) Scramble up and right to enter the shallow Main Gully. Descend this, awkward in places, to regain the top of the Alphabet Slabs.

The Chasm grabs you by the throat. React or submit. Put the boot in its right corner and jab the left foot, kung fu fashion, against the opposing wall. Surprised thus, the Chasm backs off at an open area of ledges.

Observant seconds will notice the possibility of rightward escape here; the leader must struggle to keep the party to its original intention. Persuade them by demonstrating the superb flake holds used in bypassing the ugly corner above.

A catwalk regains the upper chasm, here spanned by the Arch Tempter which preys on the lily-livered and transports them to safety. Put this prospect behind you and instead bare your knuckles for the dreaded Vertical Vice. The Vice itself grips only one leg (not too securely, it must be added) which implies there will be a gulp and pull on inferior holds before the comforting finishing jug is to hand.

If courage fails then the ungradable Subterranean Exit offers a face-saving escape. This passage into the bowels of the mountain can be found part-way up the wriggling chimney used in approaching the Vice. Disgusting it may be, but at least it's safe.

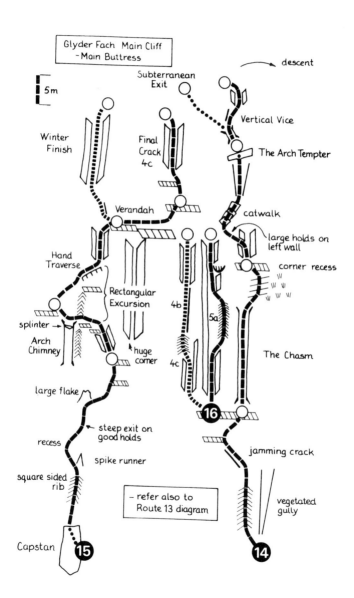

# 15: DIRECT ROUTE (S or VS) 100m

**Summary:** Energetic and absorbing climbing up the main face of Glyder Fach. The line is anything but direct. Belays and protection are good, the rock perfect. An easier finish is available for those repulsed by the formidable Final Crack. A famous but elusive classic. Illustrated on Route 14 diagram.

**First Ascent:** K. M. Ward and H. B. Gibson, April 1907.

**Best Conditions:** The cliff faces north-west at high altitude, consequently the rock is often damp during the period from autumn to spring. Allow two fine summer days after bad weather.

**Approach:** As for Route 14 to the level area above Alphabet Slabs. Walk left for 25m to a 3m block – the Capstan – which stands embedded in the terrace below the main face. 1hr.

**Starting Point:** Immediately behind the Capstan, below easy climbing leading to a small, square-sided rib with spike runner above.

**Descent:** As for Route 14 (via the summit, or scramble up and right to enter and descend Main Gully).

Each summer the Direct Route lures connoisseurs of fine climbs away from the more accessible Ogwen classics. It promises one-hundred tortuous metres of exploration as it darts and weaves among the pillars of the East Buttress. Comparisons with Chamonix granite are well-founded.

Gymnastics begin half-way up the first pitch – at a flake exit from the recess. A stance beyond occupies a ledge below a shallow chimney in the shadow of an oppressive corner. The chimney is Gibson's (*VS*), the corner Brown's (*HVS*), but neither variant is in keeping with the normal route. A Rectangular Excursion outflanks them both, beginning at the left skyline where an improbable foot ledge leads into Arch Chimney at a wedged splinter. The Hand Traverse completes the Excursion, regaining the original line above the chimney with a flurry of arms and pedalling feet.

Of the five finishes above the Verandah, those ascending from its two extremities are the most useful. By default, the easier Winter Finish makes the Hand Traverse the crux, thereby containing the overall standard to *S*. Otherwise the off-width Final Crack becomes the crux – at *VS*, a major obstacle to boots-and-rucksack traditionalists heading for the summit.

# 16: LOT'S GROOVE (VS+) & LOT'S WIFE (VS) 30m

**Summary:** Technical climbing up vertical face and corner cracks overlooking the Chasm. Adequate protection, perfect rock, exhilarating movement. Illustrated on Route 14 diagram.

**First Ascent:** Lot's Groove – C. F. Kirkus and F. E. Hicks, June 1929; Lot's Wife – C. F. Kirkus and A. M. Robinson, 1931.

**Best Conditions:** As for Route 15. Damp rock in the lower part of either route will add considerably to the difficulty.

**Approach:** As for Route 14 to a level area above Alphabet Slabs. Follow the first pitch of Route 14 to the foot of the Chasm (or scramble up Main Gully and traverse left to reach the same point). 1hr 15mins.

**Starting Point:** For either route start below the obvious slim groove just left of the Chasm.

**Descent:** (1) Scramble up left to finish up the Final Crack of Route 15 and descend as for that route.

(2) Traverse right, some scrambling, to enter Main Gully and descend this to the level area above Alphabet Slabs.

(3) Climb up to the right for a few metres until overlooking the Chasm Route catwalk (Route 14). Reverse its flaky wall and descend awkwardly over blocks to the grass break. This is about *D* standard. Finally, traverse right to enter Main Gully.

Kirkus's bold lead of Lot's Groove narrowly preceded those of Ogwen test-pieces such as Javelin Blade (Longland) and Rowan Tree Slabs (Hicks). However, those poorly protected routes retain their notoriety while the (nowadays) protectable Lot's Groove regularly finds itself on Ogwen tick lists.

Security promised by a direct ascent of the Groove proves illusory; the best line temporarily escapes its confines at about one-third height for the exposed right arête. Thus regained, the groove has something more tangible to offer in terms of holds and protection. The overhang which now looms above would be the crux, but for a fortuitous crack which splits the left wall.

The Wife makes a good follow-up to success on the Groove. As a technical problem its energetic entry groove bears comparison to anything on the parent route, but here the difficulties are shorter-lived. With this crux behind, the delightful upper jamming cracks may be enjoyed to the full.

# 17: GRIBIN CLASSICS (D, S or VS) 50m

**Summary:** A selection of popular and accessible minor classics on a sprawling outcrop near the entrance to Cwm Idwal. Ideal for a short day, or when cloud obscures the high crags.

**First Ascent:** Slab Climb – J. Laycock and S. W. Herford, May 1912; Llyn – C. H. S. R. Palmer and J. M. Edwards, July 1931; Yob Route – K. R. C. Britton and G. N. Crawshaw, August 1957; Monolith Crack – G. D. Abraham and A. P. Abraham, May 1905; Zig-Zag – S. W. Herford, J. Laycock, et al., May 1912.

**Best Conditions:** Faces north at 450m. Slab routes dry quickly in summer whereas the cracks may take another day. Without exception these routes are truly horrible when wet.

**Approach:** From Ogwen Cottage car-park (GR.649 604) on the A5 between Capel Curig and Bethesda (overspill parking near by). Follow the main Idwal path to Idwal Gate at the lakeside, and then turn sharp left to ascend directly along a fence line to the right side of the crag. Refer to Ogwen area map. GR.650 596. 20mins.

**Starting Point:** Refer to crag diagram.

**Descent:** (1) The two obvious breaks between buttresses (refer to crag diagram). Awkward in the lower reaches.
(2) The easy couloir on the far right of the crag.
(3) Llyn and Yob Route – descend Slab Climb.

Slab Climb (*D*) rarely asserts itself as a true slab. Instead, it enjoys surprisingly varied climbing, on flakes and cracks, after a devious traversing start (which is not ideal for complete beginners). There is a harder Direct Start (*VD*) for the impatient.

Llyn (*S+*) energetically climbs a crack and V-groove on Slab Climb's scarp wall. Those unfamiliar with jamming techniques may be baffled by the crux (which can be protected by large nuts).

Yob Route (*VS*) follows a longer and more serious line further left. There is little respite. It begins with a dynamic, rib sequence, and continues with a difficult corner and crack.

Monolith Crack (*S*) begins underground, but is all too open at the polished entry to the claustrophobic thrutch of the main chimney. This is no place for helmets, rucksacks or surplus flab.

Zig-Zag (*S*) remains popular despite polished holds and a bad reputation for accidents. However, care with ropework and protection adequately safeguards the crux – a smooth V-groove.

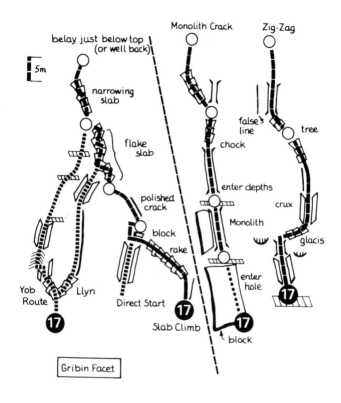

belay just below top
(or well back)

5m

narrowing
slab

flake
slab

polished
crack

Monolith Crack

Zig-Zag

chock

false
line

tree

enter depths

crux

Monolith

glacis

Yob
Route        Llyn

block
rake

block

Direct Start

Slab Climb

enter hole

enter
hole

block

Gribin Facet

descent

descent

# 18: ORDINARY ROUTE/CNEIFION ARÊTE (D) 300m

**Summary:** A long mountaineering route, nowhere difficult, impressively situated within Cwm Idwal and Cwm Cneifion. A good introduction to mountain rock. Frequent stances and protection.

**First Ascent:** Ordinary Route – T. K. Rose and C. C. B. Moss, August 1897; Cneifion Arête – G. Barlow and E. M. Barlow, 1905.

**Best Conditions:** Generally west facing at 400m to 750m. Feasible under most conditions, although the Ordinary Route resembles a fish ladder during heavy rain!

**Approach:** From Ogwen Cottage car-park (GR.649 604) on the A5 between Capel Curig and Bethesda (overspill parking near by). Follow the track into Cwm Idwal, turn left at Idwal Gate, and follow the lakeside path to the foot of the Idwal Slabs. Refer to Ogwen Area map. GR.644 589. 30mins.

**Starting Point:** Below a wide crack line which cuts the left side of the main slab frontage.

**Descent:** The Arête leads on to the Gribin Ridge:
   (1) Turn left and descend via Cwm Bochlwyd as for Route 6.
   (2) Ascend the Gribin and circle the Cwm Cneifion rim to Glyder Fawr. Descend as for Route 24.
   Descend as for Route 19 if completing only the Ordinary Route.

For most of its length the Ordinary follows a deep trough in the slab surface. Thus it is spared the characteristic insecurity of other routes here. This explains its popularity as a first climb or first lead.

After two long pitches the fault line fizzles out below an area of smoother rock. Thankfully a protectable crack splits a steep nose up which the route must exit.

Some of the moves on a scrambling finish are scarcely easier than those on the route itself. With care this section ends at a cairned shoulder from where the precarious Slabs descent enters the gully on the left. Ignoring this, the connecting route to Cneifion Arête scrambles up and left to enter Cwm Cneifion.

The Arête has a grassy front and a steep, side wall. Ignoring a possible direct entry, the first pitch starts from a worn ledge up to the right. It climbs steeply, towards the arête, before traversing first right then left, to arrive on the crest at a sandy chimney. From here the route stays close to the right edge for maximum exposure and interest – especially exciting in a gale-force wind!

Idwal Slabs & Walls

- refer to Route 24 diagram for location of upper section

- refer to Route 19 diagram for details of lower section

# 19: FAITH, HOPE & CHARITY (VD) 150m

**Summary:** Three famous climbs of enduring popularity on the unique sweep of slabs above Llyn Idwal. Polished holds, small stances, infrequent protection, and a tricky descent, create and sustain an atmosphere of unexpected seriousness.

**First Ascent:** Faith and Charity – D. R. Pye, I. A. Richards and T. Picton, April 1916; Hope – E. H. Daniell, I. A. Richards, et al., August 1915.

**Best Conditions:** North-west facing at around 450m. Much of the slab surface dries within hours of rain, particularly in summer when it catches the afternoon sun. However, drainage streaks affect some areas – particularly corners and overlaps – for a day or so after heavy rain. Climbing here in the rain is both unpleasant and precarious.

**Approach:** As for Route 18.

**Starting Point:** Refer to crag diagram.

**Descent:** This demands care, and rope protection may be advisable on some sections. Scramble up short walls and terraces to a cairned shoulder (ignore false lines which traverse left too soon). Descend a polished slab and runnel on the far side of the shoulder. Continue along a ledge to where an exposed rock descent leads down, then left (looking in) to enter the gully on the left. Either descend a series of awkward runnels close under the East Wall, or follow a diagonal path across the hillside further left.

Faith climbs the right hand facet of slabs. Often neglected in favour of more famous neighbours, it makes a good choice on busy days. Early pitches are the familiar ones of quartz veins and pockets. Interest develops with increasing height, culminating in the Cat Walk – a clean rib climbed on faith and friction.

Hope fully deserves its popularity. Although the holds are highly polished, the climbing is honest, and the greatest difficulties – the Twin Cracks – are protectable. These relent only after some insecure finger jamming and bridging unjustifiable at this standard but for a near-by runner and huge finishing flake.

Charity repels unworthy candidates at the very beginning. The shallow, parallel cracks of its first pitch are now so polished that a successful ascent warrants applause from the gallery! The scoop and shallow groove which follow are less difficult, but of course by then the ground is that much further away.

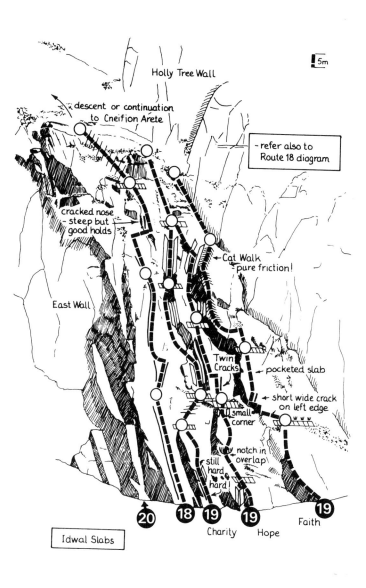

Holly Tree Wall

5m

descent or continuation
to Cneifion Arete

– refer also to
Route 18 diagram

cracked nose
– steep but
good holds

← Cat Walk
– pure friction!

East Wall

Twin
Cracks

← pocketed slab

← short wide crack
on left edge

small
corner

notch in
overlap

still
hard
hard!

20    18    19    19    19
Charity  Hope      Faith

Idwal Slabs

# 20: EAST WALL GIRDLE (S+) 175m

**Summary:** A rising traverse on bubbly rock across Idwal's dripping East Wall. Technical difficulty is not great, but small stances and poor protection make this a serious proposition for both leader and second. In combination with routes on the Holly Tree Wall (Route 21) and Upper Cliff (Route 23) it begins the finest *integrale* in Wales.

**First Ascent:** J. M. Edwards and C. H. S. R. Palmer, July 1931.

**Best Conditions:** North-east facing at 500m. The wall suffers badly from drainage; allow several fine summer days after wet weather. It rarely comes into condition between late autumn and early spring.

**Approach:** As for Route 18.

**Starting Point:** To the left of the main slab frontage below a steeper subsidiary slab (refer to Route 19 diagram). Take care not to confuse this slab with the blunt edge of the main slab frontage on the right – Tennis Shoe Direct Start (*VS*) – or the 25m rectangular slab further left – Hargreave's Slab (*S*).

**Descent:** Continue up Holly Tree Wall (Route 21) or descend as for Route 19.

The day begins inauspiciously up an inset slab. This is the notorious first pitch of Tennis Shoe (*S*), which continues up the left side of the main slabs to a trying finish below the Perched Block. Thankfully, no hold on the remainder of the route is as polished as these.

Beyond a simple quartz slab the traverse assumes its true character, crab-crawling on to the pumice cone of Heather Wall (*VS*) which it follows to a minute stance at the apex. Together they cross the concave wall and drainage streaks, but while Heather Wall veers upwards to engage its crucial bulge, the Girdle perseveres with the traverse and finally steps down to an irrigated stance below Rake End Chimney (*S*).

Impregnable walls of the Tower cast a gloomy shadow. The girdle must exploit a partial easing of their angle. There is little protection and no respite, but the small holds are reassuringly incut. The temptation now is to resolve ambiguities in route finding by escaping upwards with one of the lesser routes. That would be a mistake; the true line follows a rake to discover the wonderfully situated scooped rib of Grooved Wall (*S*), climbing it on perfect rock for an exhilarating finish.

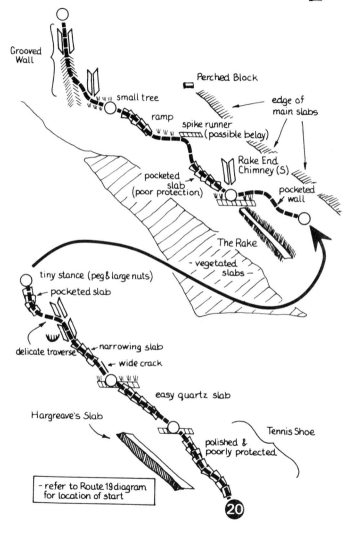

5m

Grooved Wall

Perched Block

small tree

edge of main slabs

ramp

spike runner (possible belay)

Rake End Chimney (S)

pocketed slab (poor protection)

pocketed wall

The Rake

- vegetated slabs -

tiny stance (peg & large nuts)

pocketed slab

delicate traverse

narrowing slab

wide crack

easy quartz slab

Hargreave's Slab

Tennis Shoe

polished & poorly protected

- refer to Route 19 diagram for location of start

20

# 21: HOLLY TREE WALL (VS) 45m

**Summary:** Stubborn climbs on the terminal wall of the Idwal Slabs. Individually worthwhile, but especially useful as link pitches between the Slabs (or East Wall) and Upper Cliff.

**First Ascent:** Original Route – I. A. Richards, C. F. Holland and D. E. Pilley, May 1918; Javelin Buttress – F. Graham and C. E. Jerram, April 1925.

**Best Conditions:** North-west facing at 500m. Both routes avoid main drainage lines, although comments relating to the main slab climbs (Route 19) apply equally well here.

**Approach:** As for Route 18 to the foot of the Idwal Slabs. Ascend one of the Slab or East Wall routes (Route 19 or 20) to the foot of Holly Tree Wall.

**Starting Point:** Original Route – on a terrace below the main part of the wall, at a fallen block; Javelin Buttress – at the right extremity of the terrace (care with belays here).

**Descent:** Walk left and scramble down to the cairned shoulder on the Slabs descent (Route 19). Alternatively, continue to the Upper Cliff as for the approach to Route 23.

Traditionally the Original Route gains an obvious slanting ramp via a bottomless groove which descends from its lower left end. However, the entry to this insidious scoop has baffled generations of climbers. Attempts on the gymnastic Wall Start, though no better protected, are more likely to succeed.

In contrast the ramp itself – the Crescent Slab – is both safe and enjoyable. It terminates at the hallowed site of the Holly Tree, which in earlier days lent a prickly security to attacks on the wide crack above. This crack proves untenable for short arms and tempers, so most climbers vent their frustration on the Wall Finish.

Javelin Buttress is more straightforward, but beware the pocketed slab which lures unwary victims towards the infamous Javelin Blade (*E1*). Be sure to regain the original groove line – now merely a thin crack in the wall – at superb nut and thread runners. A mantleshelf sequence beyond constitutes the crux.

No climb on the Holly Tree Wall is complete without a finale on the Continuation Wall. Here zealots queue to injure themselves on Groove Above (*S*) – the entry of which is almost as traumatic as that to Original Route – while hedonists sneak ten metres left for an incut orgy on The Arête (*VD*).

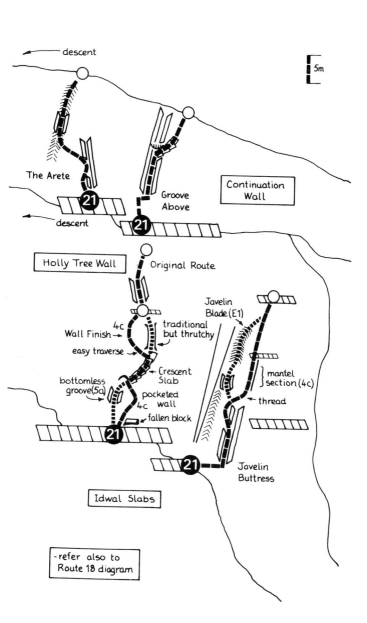

# 22: SUICIDE WALL (E2) 30m

**Summary:** A short but intimidating wall climb which involves several poorly protected moves on tiny pocket holds. Strong fingers and a calm temperament are the prerequisites of success on this historic climb. The somewhat dreary outlook is entirely appropriate.

**First Ascent:** C. Preston, R. G. Morsley and J. Haines, October 1945.

**Best Conditions:** North-east facing at 500m. A large drainage streak persists throughout bad summers, although an ascent will be possible whenever this retreats to a smear (which affects only the traverse section).

**Approach:** As for Route 18 to the lakeside path. Shortly before reaching the Idwal Slabs, strike diagonally up the grassy hillside on the left, to arrive directly below the smooth face at the upper left end of East Wall. Refer to Ogwen Area map. GR.647 588. 30mins.

**Starting Point:** Two tufts of grass indicate the half-way ledge – the most distinctive feature of the route. Start below a vague line of weakness which descends from the left side of the ledge.

**Descent:** Scramble upwards to reach a cairned shoulder, and descend as for Route 19.

Suicide Wall enjoys a reputation out of all proportion to its height and intrinsic merit. Stripped of history, it is nothing more than a potentially dangerous outcrop climb of inferior line and indifferent quality.

Satisfaction derives from the sustained application of physical skill and mental control. Modern protection makes little impression; most of the runners you see in photographs are merely thin tape slings hooked optimistically over thumb-nail flakes.

The hardest move on the route arrives almost at once, when after making an initial step up to the right, a hopeful lunge wins the temporary and painful support of a spiked pocket. Beyond this the climbing gradually eases to the half-way ledge (where the first ascent party belayed, under no illusions, to a tent peg!). It pays not to linger here for fear of dousing the adrenalin fire.

An old peg and frayed ribbon of tape protect the second crux – a tenuous sequence of moves above the right end of the ledge. After a couple of metres, a step left brings better holds and the prospect of escape along a rising rightward diagonal. Your day's work is almost done.

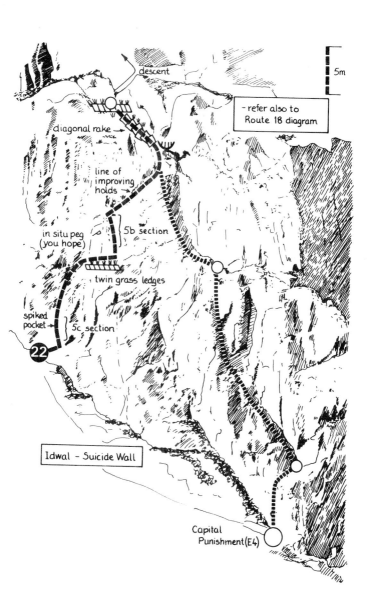

descent

diagonal rake

line of improving holds

5b section

in situ peg (you hope)

twin grass ledges

spiked pocket

5c section

22

Idwal – Suicide Wall

refer also to Route 18 diagram

5m

Capital Punishment (E4)

# 23: GREY SLAB (VS) & GREY ARÊTE (HVS) 85m

**Summary:** Climbs of undisputed excellence. A remote setting high above Cwm Idwal enhances their appeal. Grey Slab is sustained, frequently wet, and mostly unprotected. The Arête is harder but safer, with just one completely unprotected passage.

**First Ascent:** Grey Slab – J. M. Edwards and F. Reade, August 1932; Grey Arête – R. James and P. Benson, August 1959.

**Best Conditions:** Faces northwest at 800m. Grey Slab suffers badly from drainage and rarely dries completely. Grey Arête stands proud, escapes the deluge, and so dries relatively quickly – idyllic in the evening sun.

**Approach:** As for Route 18 to the foot of the Idwal Slabs. An extremely tedious direct approach ascends a scree couloir right of the Slabs (1hr 15mins). Alternatively climb Routes 20 and 21 followed by twenty minutes of scrambling, aiming to arrive at a compact cluster of ribs and slabs – the Grey Group. Refer to Route 18 diagram. GR.644 585.

**Starting Point:** Scramble up to a grass ledge below the obvious large corner between Grey Slab and Grey Arête.

**Descent:** Via the broad ridge bounding the left side of the cliff. Either descend to find terraces leading back to the start, or ascend to the summit of Glyder Fawr and descend as for Route 24.

Grey Slab begins innocently enough, but smiles fade when the leader must secure a sloping stance with a couple of poor nuts and a blunt flake. This sets the scene for the remainder of the climb.

The main slab pitch begins with a pull over an overlap to a suspect spike. This alone will protect the crux – a series of teetering moves left across a shallow rib on minute incuts. An optimistic step-up ends at a good hold on which to hang tattered nerves (though not, alas, a tape runner). Retreat being out of the question, it is a great relief to discover a line of holds extending up to and across a wet patch to runners at the top overlap.

Grey Arête begins innocently too, rearing its head only at the second pitch – a pocketed wall of some delicacy and no protection. It ends at a good ledge but the confident leader will spurn this temporary haven and embark immediately on the crucial (but protected) cracked arête, thus completing in one swipe the finest elevated pitch in the Ogwen Valley.

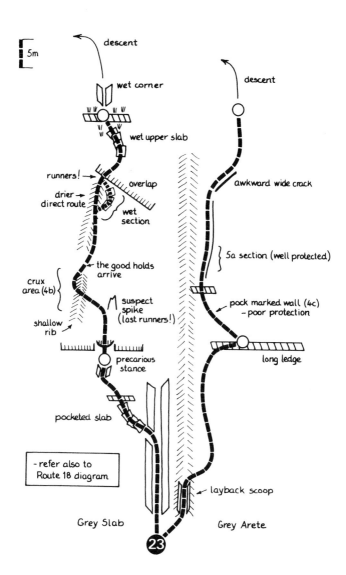

5m

descent

wet corner

descent

wet upper slab

runners!

overlap

awkward wide crack

drier → direct route

wet section

5a section (well protected)

the good holds arrive

crux area (4b)

suspect spike (last runners!)

pock marked wall (4c) – poor protection

shallow rib

precarious stance

long ledge

pocketed slab

- refer also to Route 18 diagram

layback scoop

Grey Slab

Grey Arete

23

# 24: CLOGWYN DU GULLY (III or IV) 100m

**Summary:** A short gully, often in condition, which emerges near the summit of Glyder Fawr.

**First Ascent:** Winter (Right Hand Branch) – O. G. Jones and party, 1899; Left Hand Branch – unknown.

**Best Conditions:** Faces north-east at 900m. Water-ice or deep snow are by themselves unhelpful – a gradual build-up of both produces the best conditions.

**Approach:** As for Route 18 to Llyn Idwal. Leave the lakeside path and ascend diagonally across the hillside to enter lower Cwm Cneifion. The crag stands on the right of the head wall in the upper cwm. Refer to Ogwen Area map. GR.647 582. 1hr 30mins in good conditions.

**Starting Point:** The gully defines the right side of the main face. Start at the lowest point of the crag.

**Descent:** (1) Circle the rim of Cwm Cneifion leftwards and descend the Gribin Ridge as for Route 6.

(2) Descend the path on the north-west slope of Glyder Fawr (unpleasant scree in summer, insecure open snow or ice slopes in winter) to Llyn y Cwn (GR.637 584). Follow a path north-eastwards from the lake and descend the Kitchen Cliffs (refer to crag diagram).

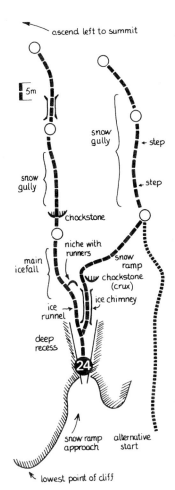

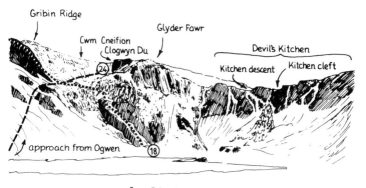

Gribin Ridge
Glyder Fawr
Cwm Cneifion
Clogwyn Du
Devil's Kitchen
Kitchen descent
Kitchen cleft
(24)
approach from Ogwen
(18)

Cwm Idwal

Blown powder swirls and settles in the great bowl of Cwm Cneifion during severe winters, obscuring all but the sharpest rib of rock. Snow lingers here long after spring thaws have scoured other high cwms, preserving a number of worthwhile grade / exits. The grim facet of Clogwyn Du also survives.

Sometimes a preliminary pitch guards entrance to the gully. In a good winter, however, most of this will be lost beneath drifts and the first stance will be taken within the confines of the gully itself. The division comes almost at once: the Left Hand Branch bridges the left corner and takes to a steep ice pitch on the wall; the Right Hand Branch tackles a chimney and chockstone directly ahead. Those going left will have their exit complicated by chockstones, while those going right – assuming the depth of snow permits the awkward exit from the chockstone – will be rewarded by a straightforward snow gully.

Since the approach to Clogwyn Du is far too long to come away empty handed, a direct grade *II/III* entry to the upper gully of Right Hand Branch may save the day when borderline conditions prevail.

# 25: SOUTH GULLY (IV) 115m

**Summary:** The classic Idwal ice climb. It retains some of the atmosphere of a gully even though most of the climbing takes place on open ice-falls. Stances and belays are good, although protection depends almost entirely on screws. Steep but never overbearing.

**First Ascent:** Winter – probably J. Brown and R. Moseley, 1952.

**Best Conditions:** Requires up to ten days of consistently low temperatures to form fully (normally this occurs at least once each winter). Occasionally, the true bed of the gully banks up with snow, to give a less demanding climb.

**Approach:** As for Route 18 to the Idwal Slabs. Continue diagonally rightwards, crossing a rocky stream bed (which in its higher reaches provides an excellent grade *III* practice climb, often in condition). Leave the path after a further 100m and ascend a snow couloir, or its flanking scree or snow slopes, directly to the foot of the gully. Refer to Ogwen Area map. GR.641 587. 45mins.

**Starting Point:** Below the lower ice-fall.

**Descent:** Ascend the easy upper gully, then contour right to descend the ramp of the Devil's Kitchen path (refer to crag drawing).

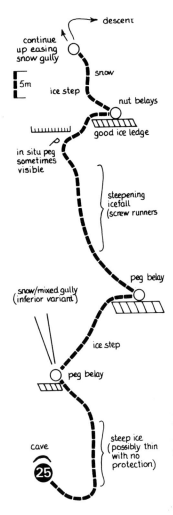

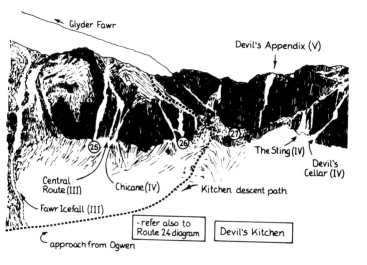

Glyder Fawr

Devil's Appendix (V)

The Sting (IV)

Devil's Cellar (IV)

Central Route (III)

Chicane (IV)

Kitchen descent path

Fawr Icefall (III)

- refer also to Route 24 diagram

Devil's Kitchen

approach from Ogwen

Ice-falls are subject to a curious visual aberration. Viewed from the approach they appear vertical; from beneath, slabby. As you would expect their actual inclinations lie somewhere between the two. Psychologically this is devastating – the initial sense of terror, temporarily dispelled on arrival, returns the instant the first pick is planted. This explains why several climbers can usually be found hiding in the cave left of the first ice pitch of South Gully.

Under ideal conditions the entry pitch forms into a substantial boss of chewy water-ice. Thwack, thwack, and it's done. More usually, having already had seven bells knocked out of it the previous weekend, you will find yourself wobbling unprotected up something as tangible as a net curtain.

All being well, the alternating leader will find pegs and a cosy belay (in winter terms) below the main ice-fall and the big lead. Here rocks entombed by the frozen wave threaten to deflect screws and blunt the tips of panic-driven tools, but having got this far the depth of ice should entice you ever upwards. No need to worry if the flow narrows and steepens at the spout – your eyes will melt a furrow to the summit.

# 26: THE RAMP (II/III) & THE SCREEN (IV) 120m & 60m

**Summary:** Neighbouring water-ice climbs on the accessible head wall of Cwm Idwal. Often in condition during periods of severe cold. The Screen includes a short vertical section and relies almost entirely on screws for belays and protection.

**First Ascent:** Not known.

**Best Conditions:** A leaning wall shields much of the Ramp from snowfall; despite a relatively gentle angle it remains essentially an ice climb. A ribbon of ice may appear after only a few days of subzero temperatures, although it can be quite difficult in these borderline conditions. The Screen takes much longer to form properly. Note that huge icicles begin falling at the onset of thaw, and threaten to impale unfortunate seconds strapped to the lower stances!

**Approach:** As for Route 25 but continue along the path, almost to the Kitchen Cleft entrance.

**Starting Point:** At a runnel below the lowest ice wall of The Screen.

**Descent:** Both routes emerge on the ramp of the Devil's Kitchen path. Follow this down to the right, to regain the foot of the cliffs.

Devil's Kitchen ice climbing is the winter equivalent of outcropping at Tremadog. No need for rucksacks and summits here. Groups of climbers sit eating lunch below the crag, watching the action and wondering if there's time for 'a quicky' before dark.

The Ramp has a lot to recommend it as an introduction to water-ice, but the Screen is undoubtedly the major prize. An initial wall is optional – the ice ledge it gains may be reached by a walk from the right – but psychologically it is important preparation for the vertical section which follows.

Sometimes the crux forms as a groove, gratefully bridged. More usually it fills out as a stepped wall, complete with fragile mushrooms. After a few metres it falls back as a slabby scoop leading into the ice grotto. Steps cut into its floor relieve aching calf muscles, but the clutch of ice screws brings no lasting peace of mind.

After tinkling through a brittle veil of ice fingers, the final pitch traverses a ramp to discover a bridging corner. Prolong the agony of your belayer in the grotto by disclosing none of this; let him deduce what he can from your muffled grunts and from the hesitant pull of the rope.

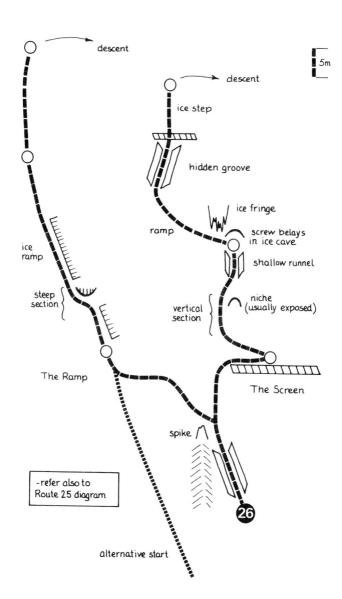

descent

descent

5m

ice step

hidden groove

ice fringe

ramp

screw belays
in ice cave

ice
ramp

shallow runnel

steep
section

niche
(usually exposed)

vertical
section

The Ramp

The Screen

spike

-refer also to
Route 25 diagram

26

alternative start

# 27: DEVIL'S KITCHEN (VD+) & DEVIL'S STAIRCASE (S) 90m

**Summary:** Routes of great character on the rotting arc of cliffs beyond Llyn Idwal. Rock deep within the Kitchen Cleft is unreliable and permanently wet. Atmosphere is everything. In contrast the chimney/gully line of the Staircase produces surprisingly clean and enjoyable climbing, culminating in a classic squeeze chimney.

**First Ascent:** Kitchen – W. R. Reade and W. P. McCulloch, May 1898; Staircase – O. G. Jones and G. D. Abraham, Easter 1899.

**Best Conditions:** The Staircase carries a moderate amount of drainage and rarely dries completely (a grade easier in those conditions). The Kitchen never dries but is best avoided after heavy rain, when climbers and other loose debris will be flushed from the Cleft.

**Approach:** As for Route 25, but continue along the diagonal path to the Kitchen Cleft entrance. Refer to Ogwen Area map and Route 25 diagram. GR.639 588. 45mins.

**Starting Point:** Kitchen: scramble up the bed of the Cleft to where a huge boulder bars further progress. Staircase: a terrace extends rightwards from the Cleft entrance – follow it until below the first major fault line.

**Descent:** Walk left above the line of cliffs to join the Devil's Kitchen path. Follow its slanting ramp to regain the start.

The walls of the Kitchen Cleft converge. A great boulder spans the gap – the Waterfall Pitch. Water gushes from beneath, cascades down the right edge, but merely dribbles over the left wall. It succumbs to swearing or combined tactics.

Beyond lies the inner sanctuary, illuminated by the narrow slit of sky. On the right is a slender pinnacle – a pulpit overlooking the altar where lambs, sacrificed from the world above, come to rest. The waterfall plays the Devil's tune, muddling thoughts with its pounding beat.

Salvation lies up a bulging crack on the left wall. It gradually eases until a more open crack continues the escape. Some have belayed at the ledge beyond, but the rusty pegs crumble at your touch and it seems best to go on. A traverse line to the capstone reveals itself, protected by tottering spikes. Far below your second awaits the outcome, eyes aflame with Devil worship.

The Devil's Staircase is more conventional!

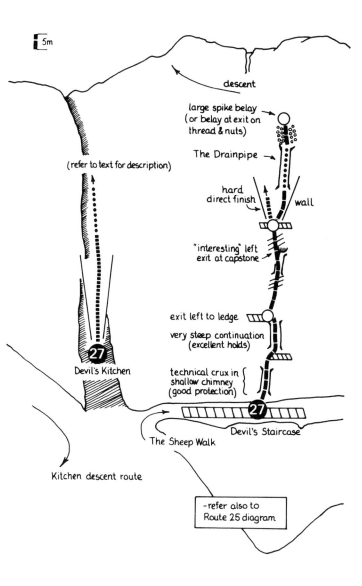

# Llanberis Pass Area

The Pass has become famous for short, hard climbs on south facing roadside crags – Grochan, Wastad, Cromlech. Although most of the routes selected from the north side of the Pass belong to this category, several among them have been drawn from the lower grades. Flying Buttress, perhaps the easiest route in the Pass, is also one of its finest. Of the harder routes, the trio of climbs on the Cromlech central walls – Left Wall, Cenotaph Corner and Cemetery Gates – are now legendary. Every career-minded climber will place these routes high on the hit list.

The shady south side of the Pass is a microcosm of Welsh climbing. Every type of climb is represented. Some of these routes are outstanding, and climbers will rightly travel the length of Britain for an opportunity to attempt the Direct Route, Diagonal, Main Wall, or The Grooves.

**Approaches:** All routes described in this section can be approached from the A4086 between Pen y Pass and Llanberis. A bus route serves Nant Peris (via Caernarfon), about 2km walk from the main crags. In summer, the Sherpa bus service operates between Nant Peris and Pen y Gwryd (connections to Capel Curig and Beddgelert).

**Accommodation:** *Camping*: Gwastadnant, 4km east of Llanberis near A4086 (GR.610 579); Blaen y Nant, opposite Carreg Wastad (GR.623 568); unofficial and discouraged roadside sites between Pont y Gromlech and Clogwyn y Grochan.
*High camps/bivouacs*: Cromlech Boulders, near Pont y Gromlech (for roadside crags); and Cwm Glas (for Cyrn Las etc.)
*Bunkhouse/barns*: Opposite the campsite in Gwastadnant. Several climbing clubs have huts in the valley.
*Youth Hostels*: Llanberis and Pen y Pass.
*Hotels/B&B*: Hotels plus numerous B&B houses in Llanberis and Nant Peris. Hotel at Pen y Gwryd.

**Services:** Nant Peris has a pub, general store, and telephone. Llanberis has the usual small town amenities, including an equipment shop. At Pen y Pass there are toilets and a café.

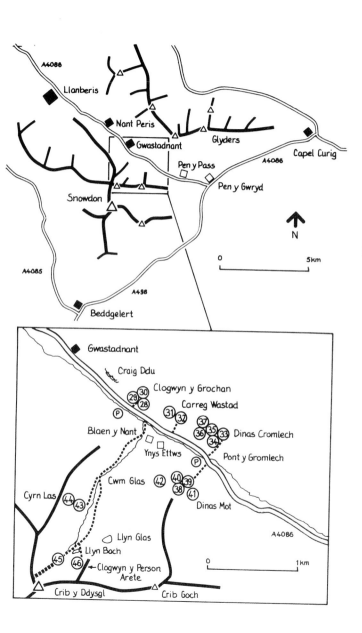

Final pitch on Cemetery Gates (Route 34), Dinas Cromlech.

The Hand Traverse on Direct Route (Route 39), Dinas Mot.

# 28: BRANT (VS) & BRANT DIRECT (VS+) 115m & 25m

**Summary:** A devious route which, none the less, secures the easiest line up a very steep wall. The upper section loses itself among ribs and terraces. The Direct Start, a sustained bridging problem, makes a worthwhile climb in itself (abseil descent). Double ropes are an advantage on the normal route.

**First Ascent:** J. M. Edwards and J. E. Q. Barford, August 1940. Direct Start – P. R. J. Harding, April 1949.

**Best Conditions:** The wall faces south at low altitude but carries hillside drainage. Upper slabs remain damp for a few days after bad weather, and in that condition are both difficult and insecure.

**Approach:** Ascend directly up scree and boulders from the lay-by. Refer to Llanberis Area map. GR.621 572. 5mins.

**Starting Point:** Below the Central Wall (refer to diagram for precise locations).

**Descent:** Via the left bounding gully of Goats Buttress. Go left along the cliff top to the finger stone which identifies the short, but awkward, initial descent chimney (may be difficult to locate at first visit). Continue carefully down slabs and enter the water-worn gully. Exit left (looking out), when possible, to descend short walls and terraces. For the Direct Start, either continue as for the normal route, or traverse right to make an abseil descent from holly trees.

Slaty rock and unremitting verticality are the hallmarks of routes on Clogwyn y Grochan's lower Central Wall. Brant is no exception. Its crucial first pitch, a rising traverse, terrorises nervous seconds.

The V-chimney baffles some climbers, while admitting others at first thrutch. It wipes superior smiles from the faces of leaders approaching via the Direct! Landmarks thereafter become progressively less distinct. Route finding beyond the band of overlapping slabs is almost arbitrary. A pedantic leader will be paralysed by his inability to distinguish between yew trees 'small', 'large' and 'ancient'. It seems best simply to choose the most promising line and follow it skywards through the greenery.

The Direct Start, an emphatic V-groove, suffers no such ambiguities. Once graded *Extremely Severe*, modern protection now permits the *VS* leader to experiment with wide bridging and jamming in comparative safety.

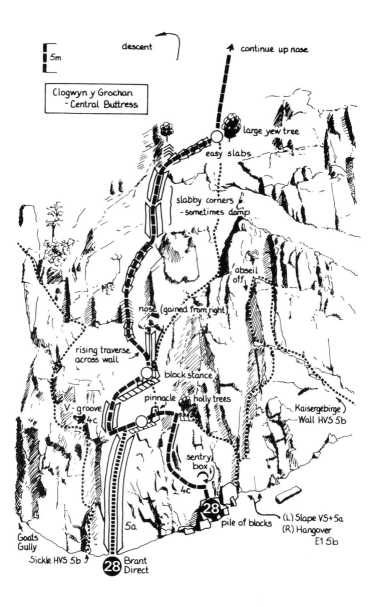

descent

continue up nose

5m

Clogwyn y Grochan
- Central Buttress

large yew tree

easy slabs

slabby corners
- sometimes damp

abseil
off

nose (gained from right)

rising traverse
across wall

block stance

pinnacle

holly trees

V - groove
4c

Kaisergebirge
Wall HVS 5b

sentry
box

4c

28

pile of blocks

(L) Slape VS+ 5a
(R) Hangover
E1 5b

Goats
Gully

5a

28   Brant
Direct

Sickle HVS 5b

# 29: NEA (S+) 75m

**Summary:** Moderately interesting climbing following the best line up a sunny roadside crag. Very popular. Bad communications and rope drag plague the long first pitch. Major difficulties can be adequately protected.

**First Ascent:** N. E. Morin and J. M. Edwards, September 1941.

**Best Conditions:** South facing at low altitude. Goats Buttress stands proud from the remainder of the crag and is therefore spared its drainage problems, but in winter corner cracks may remain damp for a day or so after rain.

**Approach:** Ascend directly up scree and boulders from the lay-by. Refer to Llanberis Area map. GR.621 572. 5mins.

**Starting Point:** On a large corner ledge, about 20m above the lowest point of the buttress (accessed via an easy chimney on the left).

**Descent:** Traverse left along grass terraces to join the descent from Route 28 below its chimney.

Nea's starting ledge feels comparatively secluded, divorced from frenetic activity on Central Wall towards which the binoculars of picnicking voyeurs are normally trained. This will soon change. Forced at once from the main corner line, your staccato progress up the cracked left wall soon begins to attract attention. As well it might. An overhang forces a teetering (but protected) return around the nose into a wide corner crack where you may hide for a while.

It was this distinctive central section of the climb that had caught the eye of Menlove Edwards prior to the first ascent. He had invited his companion, Nea Morin, to 'have a look at it', which she duly did. Moments before, she had narrowly escaped having to follow Menlove up the evil Goats Gully (luckily he had been repulsed by the entry) and doubtless was pleased to accept this far more attractive offer. Thirty five years later Nea Morin repeated the climb with her daughter and grandson, by which time it had become one of the most popular climbs in the Pass.

Early in 1984 the original top pitch – a cracked corner, yellow and decaying – collapsed. It was a nasty piece of work and no great loss to the crag (although Nea Morin, doubtless influenced by Menlove's penchant for rotten rock, had found it 'excellent . . . and immensely satisfying'!). As it is, the top pitch of Spectre, intimidating but fair, barely increases the standard of the original.

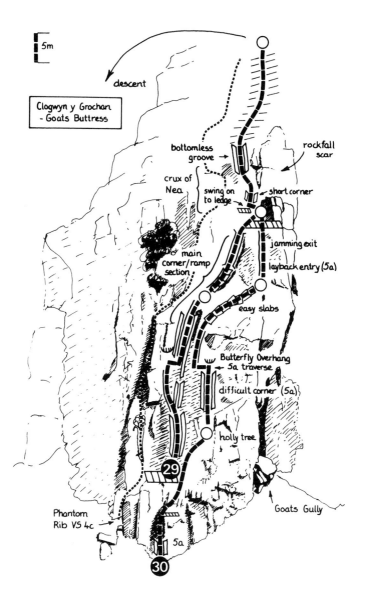

5m

descent

Clogwyn y Grochan
- Goats Buttress

bottomless groove

rockfall scar

crux of Nea

swing on to ledge

short corner

jamming exit

main corner/ramp section

layback entry (5a)

easy slabs

Butterfly Overhang
5a traverse

difficult corner (5a)

holly tree

29

Phantom Rib VS 4c

Goats Gully

5a

30

# 30: SPECTRE (HVS) 90m

**Summary:** Continually interesting climbing, up grooves and cracks, on the clean face of Goats Buttress. Its three crucial pitches, including a delicate traverse and strenuous jamming crack, will succumb only to a determined approach. Good protection (*see* Route 29 diagram).

**First Ascent:** P. R. J. Harding and E. H. Phillips, May 1947.

**Best Conditions:** Faces south at low altitude and therefore dries quickly after rain.

**Approach:** Ascend directly up scree and boulders from the lay-by. Refer to Llanberis Area map. GR.621 572. 5mins.

**Starting Point:** At the lowest point of Goats Buttress, below a slim crack.

**Descent:** Traverse left, along grass terraces, to join the descent from Route 28 below its chimney.

Peter Harding steered Welsh climbing through a transitional period from pre-war *VS* to post-war *Extreme*. Today, his climbs seem only fractionally more difficult than the top routes of the previous era; but at the time they were a definite step forward.

Harding and Phillips had spotted the line of Spectre while making the second ascent of Brant (in nailed boots). Harding claims their estimate of the route promised a pleasant outing at *V.Diff* standard! They attempted it the following day, but were forced to revise their estimate by several grades.

An overhang confronted Harding on the second pitch. He placed a peg (carrying pegs on prospective *V.Diffs*!), but on this occasion failed to find a direct solution. Instead, he traversed delicately left, and forced an exit on to a band of easy slabs.

In 1947 the fearsome upper crack, now a clean if strenuous jamming exercise, had been choked with vegetation. Harding talks of finding 'a nice bunch of lupin-like plants in the back of the crack', but he did not judge them safe enough to use as handholds and instead made do with 'a well-executed series of thrutches'.

Spectre quickly gained a reputation as the hardest route in the Pass. And so it remained until Joe Brown climbed Hangover on the same crag in 1951 – coincidentally, a line Harding and Phillips had attempted on the day prior to their Spectre ascent. Today their 'V.Diff' climb on Goats Buttress takes its rightful place in the Llanberis honours list between Brant and Cemetery Gates.

# 31: WRINKLE (VD) 75m

**Summary:** One of the few worthwhile climbs at this standard in the Pass, and therefore extremely popular. A serious outing by any criteria, but especially because of loose rock splinters lodged within the shattered flutings which are so typical of the crag. Poor protection on the upper slabby section. Illustrated on Route 32 crag diagram.

**First Ascent:** M. P. Ward, J. E. Q. Barford and B. Pierre, 1947.

**Best Conditions:** The crag faces south-west at low altitude and escapes most of the hillside drainage. The route will dry quickly after a summer shower, although local drainage may affect its top pitch for a day or more in winter or after prolonged bad weather (note that the top pitch is especially insecure in those conditions).

**Approach:** Direct from lay-bys in the Llanberis Pass as for Route 32.

**Starting Point:** Below a boss of rock on the left side of the crag, just left of a large shallow recess in the wall. (Refer to Route 32 crag diagram.)

**Descent:** Traverse left along terraces (one awkward step) to enter and descend the rock-filled gully on the left side of the crag.

Newcomers to the Pass invariably congregate at Carreg Wastad. Superficially it resembles the Ogwen outcrops of Bochlwyd Buttress or Gribin Facet, and like them has been spared the patronage of 'rock-jocks' who prefer to flex their muscles and colourful tights on the walls of the Grochan or Cromlech. The Wastad is a half-way house for the uninitiated.

Wrinkle's initial wall, reputedly straightforward, proves disconcertingly steep and polished. An off-balance traverse, which follows, merely reinforces the growing sense of unease. A large oak once thrived on the ledge beyond, welcoming; but that was before trampling boot soles eroded the last of its rooting compound. The stance is now a good deal more exposed than it once was.

A wide crack looks promising but most quit it for ledges on the right wall, returning up the first of several fluted slabs to a bay stance. The final pitch consumes the wrinkled slab in a single, lonely run-out on which spaced protection and suspect rock increase tension but intensify experience. Rain reinforces the effect.

# 32: CRACKSTONE RIB (S) 55m

**Summary:** A famous classic, much sought after by newcomers to the Pass. Exposed positions – notably those on the crucial rib – are the main attraction. Protection is merely adequate. A curious organ-pipe structure ensures that some areas of rock remain worryingly loose, regardless of how much debris has been excavated in the past. A stance near the rib edge is traditional, but requires extra care with belays.

**First Ascent:** J. M. Edwards and J. B. Joyce, July 1935.

**Best Conditions:** South-west facing at low altitude. Dries quickly after rain, summer or winter (within hours on a windy day).

**Approach:** From lay-bys in the Llanberis Pass. Ascend directly to the lowest point of the crag (or more pleasantly by a grassy rib on the right followed by a leftward traverse). Refer to Llanberis Area map. GR.626 570. 10mins.

**Starting Point:** On grass terraces a few metres below the foot of a larger corner central to the cliff.

**Descent:** As for Route 31 (down the left-hand gully), or down the steep grass couloir on the right of the crag.

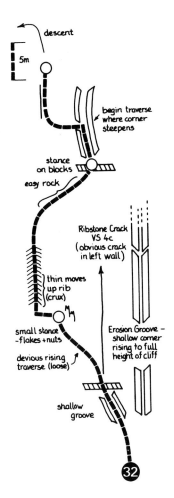

descent

5m

begin traverse where corner steepens

stance on blocks

easy rock

Ribstone Crack VS 4c (obvious crack in left wall)

thin moves up rib (crux)

small stance – flakes + nuts

Erosion Groove – shallow corner rising to full height of cliff

devious rising traverse (loose)

shallow groove

32

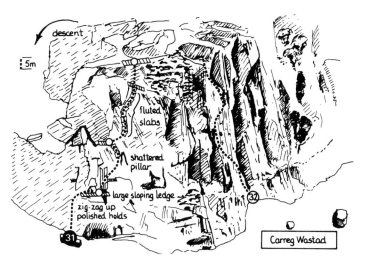

descent

5m

fluted
slabs

shattered
pillar

large sloping ledge

zig-zag up
polished holds

31

32

Carreg Wastad

A ragged crack splits the right wall of the rib. The first pitch climbs straight up a shallow groove towards it, but then has second thoughts and veers left towards the rib. This direct line is Ribstone Crack, a well-protected but fierce *VS*.

The line of the diagonal traverse stands out even from the road. In this case the band of pale rock is not evidence of chalk abuse, but of decades of enthusiastic removal of loose rock! Situations on the traverse progressively become more exposed, culminating in arrival at a tiny stance adjacent to the rib. Here good nuts on the left supplement a sheaf of highly suspect flakes. Without them no one of sound mind could bear to witness the leader's execution of the crux – a balance sequence supported by polished nubbins.

The upper stance is palatial by comparison. Here the second will curl up with a good book (this one?), while his indecisive leader ponders the choice of two traverse lines, both of which access the finishing crack with its mildly puzzling entry.

Crackstone Rib may not be the finest route in the Pass, but it does have a certain tumbledown charm. Tread gently.

## 33: FLYING BUTTRESS (D+) 100m

**Summary:** A superb climb, one of the best in Wales. Interest develops quickly, and is sustained in the quest for the key exit chimney. The rock is mostly reliable, if badly polished. The upper section demands thoughtful ropework and a steady second.

**First Ascent:** J. M. Edwards, December 1931.

**Best Conditions:** South facing at an altitude of 400m. The ridge carries no drainage and therefore dries quickly. In the final chimney, however, water streaks may persist for some days after rain.

**Approach:** From the lay-by near Pont y Gromlech. Ascend scree and heather towards the right-hand side of the crag (some awkward steps). Refer to Llanberis Area map. GR.629 569. 25mins.

**Starting Point:** Below a subsidiary ridge (the Flying Buttress), at the upper right end of the crag.

**Descent:** Scramble down to a col between Cromlech summit and the hillside behind. Cross the col and enter a steep gully which defines the right side of the crag. Leave it almost at once for heathery steps on the left (looking out), and descend with some scrambling to the foot of the climb.

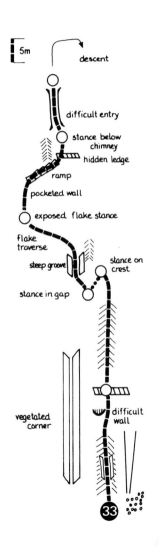

By nature, most good climbs in the Pass will be graded *VS* or harder. That is the price of escaping vegetated fault lines. More rarely a route of moderate difficulty ventures on to steep rock, linking an unlikely series of holds to produce climbing of exceptional quality. Flying Buttress is such a route.

Unusually for the Pass, the route begins on a ridge complete with jugs, spillikins and polished footholds. It could be Ogwen, were it not for those nagging doubts over rock quality which add hesitancy to movement. A problem wall below the half-way ledge adds a spark of technical interest.

A draughty notch between ridge and impending upper buttress is the turning point (some take this literally and turn right for the scree slopes and an early lunch!). Exposure snaps at your heels as you traverse the flake, to what the pioneers would have called 'an airy perch'. The next pitch begins up a series of pockets, but the line is soon deflected by a rightward ramp line. Finally, it stutters to a halt below the exit chimney. Ultimate success now depends on just one pull, slither, squirm, graunch and grimace. It brings tears to your eyes.

# 34: CEMETERY GATES (E1) 55m

**Summary:** Intimidating and exposed climbing up the cracked right arête of Cenotaph Corner. Good protection eases the strain of successive commitments to fingery wall climbing.

**First Ascent:** J. Brown and D. Whillans, September 1951.

**Best Conditions:** South-west facing at an altitude of 400m. The arête is exposed to drying winds, but crack seepage will affect the lower section in the period after prolonged wet weather. Catches the sun from mid-morning to dusk.

**Approach:** From the lay-by near Pont y Gromlech. Ascend scree and heather leading up to the right-hand side of the crag, and then trend left towards its centre. Finally, scramble up a well-worn leftward diagonal line, to arrive at ledges below the huge central corner. Refer to Llanberis Area map. GR.629 569. 25mins.

**Starting Point:** Traverse right, and descend a crack to reach a secluded stance among trees below the right arête of the corner.

**Descent:** (1) Abseil down Right Wall from a tree a few metres right of Cenotaph Corner.
(2) Continue left along the Valley, crossing above Cenotaph Corner, to ascend a diagonal crack and short walls to the summit of the Cromlech. Descend as for Route 33.

Brown and Whillans borrowed the name Cemetery Gates from the destination board of a Chester bus. That was in 1951 and the words have lost none of their poignancy in the interim. Brown and Whillans had to fight for this one, and so will you.

The big pitch begins up the right side of the arête, crossing below a small overhang to gain the main crack line with a difficult move. At the next hard move a good nut threatens to occupy the superior finger slot, but common sense prevails. Cruelly, the crux arrives a couple of metres below the Girdle ledge, just as quivering fingers are threatening to uncurl. Assuming success, what few nuts remain on the rack may now be stuffed into cracks left, right and centre, to secure this most exposed of stances.

The second follows with white knuckles and bulging eyes, finally grabbing your ankle to complete the move on to the ledge. Now is the time to break the news that leading through would be the wise thing to do. Mutter something about wobbly belay pegs if your suggestion meets with any resistance.

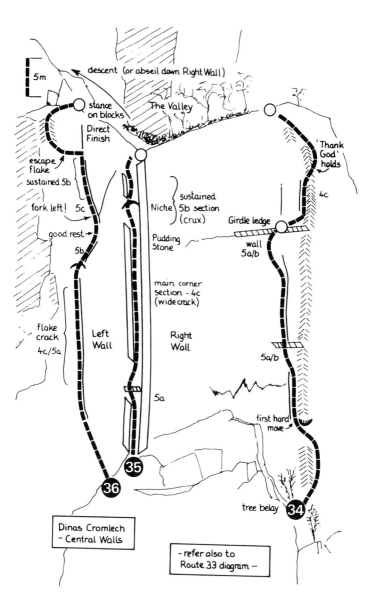

5m

descent (or abseil down Right Wall)

stance on blocks

The Valley

Direct Finish

escape flake

sustained 5b

fork left! 5c

good rest →

5b

flake crack

4c/5a

Left Wall

Right Wall

'Thank God' holds

4c

sustained 5b section (crux)

Niche

Girdle ledge

Pudding Stone

wall 5a/b

main corner section - 4c (wide crack)

5a

5a/b

first hard move →

36

35

34

tree belay

Dinas Cromlech - Central Walls

- refer also to Route 33 diagram -

# 35: CENOTAPH CORNER (E1) 40m

**Summary:** The most celebrated rock climb in Wales. Technicalities are concentrated in a hard move at 6m, and within an extended crux sequence entering and leaving the Niche a few metres below the top. Some essential holds have become polished; the route now represents the upper limit of this grade. No aid required. Excellent protection, mostly from average-sized nuts. Attracts heavy traffic during settled weather. Illustrated on Route 34 diagram.

**First Ascent:** J. Brown and D. Belshaw, August 1952.

**Best Conditions:** The corner is often damp, despite its southerly aspect and moderate altitude (400m). Large drainage streaks appear on the right wall after bad weather and persist for several days. On fine summer weekends, start early to avoid queues (some leaders like to make a day of it!).

**Approach:** As for Route 34.

**Starting Point:** At the foot of the corner. (Where else?)

**Descent:** (1) Abseil down Right Wall from a sturdy tree in the Valley.
(2) Ascend a diagonal crack on the left, and continue up short walls to the summit of the Cromlech. Descend as for Route 33.

A rich history adds texture to the drama of climbing the Corner. The three great pioneers of the Pass each played a part: Menlove Edwards 'discovered' the cliff and named the corner; Peter Harding made several unsuccessful attempts; and Joe Brown completed the first lead – though not before a nearly disastrous attempt, when he dropped a peg hammer on to his second's head. We note in passing that Joe Brown climbed in socks, during the successful attempt, to improve friction in the poor conditions.

The climbing is surprisingly varied for a corner of such geometric regularity – bridging, jamming, laybacking (thankfully not much of that) and wall climbing are all represented. None fail to be impressed by the setting within these two great walls, but some will underestimate the difficulties. Failures are not uncommon. Three sections demand respect: a leftward swing and pull up from a layback position at 6m; an insecure exit from an off-width crack to enter the Niche at 30m; and a bridging sequence to leave the Niche a few metres below the top. A few leaders, doubtless startled by their unexpected progress, have fallen from the final move – a finger pull on the left wall.

# 36: LEFT WALL (E2) 40m

**Summary:** Magnificent climbing, in a single run-out, up the left wall of Cenotaph Corner. Difficulties steadily increase, culminating in a precarious finger crack high on the route. Excellent protection throughout, although attempts to lace the crux will drain strength and invite a fall. No aid required. Hard for the grade. Illustrated on Route 34 diagram.

**First Ascent:** As a partial aid route – R. Moseley, J. Smith and J. Sutherland, May 1956.

**Best Conditions:** South-east facing at moderate altitude (400m) and therefore dries quickly after a shower (but oozes water for a day or so after prolonged rain).

**Approach:** As for Route 34 to the foot of Cenotaph Corner.

**Starting Point:** On a glacis a few metres below the corner, where holds lead up left past a spike to the start of an obvious crack splitting the left wall.

**Descent:** (1) Scramble up short walls and corners on the left, to gain the summit of the Cromlech. Descend to the right of the crag, as for Route 33.
(2) Scramble up to the right for a few metres, then reverse a diagonal crack to the Valley. Abseil down Right Wall from the best of the trees a few metres right of Cenotaph Corner.

Large holds in the initial crack foster indiscipline. Boisterous climbing replaces slow cunning. A dog-leg right brings the flake crack to hand; frisky layaways demolish it in seconds. An inner voice counsels restraint, but runners continue to flop into place with clockwork regularity, so why worry?

At a tiny niche, the crack bends right and narrows to an unhelpful slit. Wall footholds disappear at the same time. Support from a finger pocket seems pathetic after the handfuls of flake recently quitted. Only the prospect of a hands-off rest, on the ledge beyond, encourages.

The crack forks: right for Resurrection, left for Left Wall. Forking crack. Wires protect hard moves towards improving holds. Time to regret squandered stamina. Fly-on-the-wall exposure, exhilarating at the flake crack, suddenly becomes sickening. A quiet descends on the gathering below the Corner, their eyes upturned and expectant. Among them your second twitches nervously – for once braced and attentive. In a few seconds your fingertips could be curling over the escape flake. Might as well go for it.

# 37: DIVES/BETTER THINGS (S+) 65m

**Summary:** Two contrasting pitches – each of sustained interest – combined to produce the best climb, at this standard, on the north side of the Pass. Straightforward to anyone proficient at jamming and bridging, otherwise strenuous and intimidating. Major difficulties are well protected.

**First Ascent:** Dives – J. M. Edwards, December 1931; Better Things – T. D. Bourdillon, April 1949,

**Best Conditions:** South-west facing at moderate altitude (400m). Seepage from beneath the big roof drains continually across the rising traverse of the first pitch. Fortunately, this section is not too difficult. The upper crack will remain damp for a day or so after prolonged bad weather.

**Approach:** From the lay-by near Pont y Gromlech. Ascend scree and heather towards the right-hand side of the crag, and then traverse unstable scree to arrive at ledges below its left side. Refer to Llanberis Area map. GR.629 569. 20mins.

**Starting Point:** Below the left end of a prominent diagonal roof. Refer to Route 33 crag drawing for general location.

**Descent:** (1) Scramble up left then right to the Cromlech summit and descend as for Route 33.
(2) Less satisfactorily, down the left bounding gully of the crag (a short chimney to finish – hard to find).

First objective is the slabby, but treeless, haven known as the Forest. The journey to reach it begins with a brutally overhanging crack, climbed quickly on improving holds. Beyond this a diagonal roof, black and dripping, forces a rising rightward traverse over pumice-textured rock.

The Forest serves as a mid-term clearing house for this part of the cliff. The final test of Sabre Cut – a poorly protected corner – is responsible for more than a few drop-outs. For them, the choice is between Dives without honours (the ordinary finish), or back to school with Spiral Stairs.

All this is of only academic interest if you expect Better Things above. From a foothold stance you will enter the V-groove directly, generating maximum thrust for the crux. A string of runners tossed into the crack at regular intervals will act like a ratchet to prevent downward slippage. Mechanical it may be, but it beats free-falling down Sabre Cut!

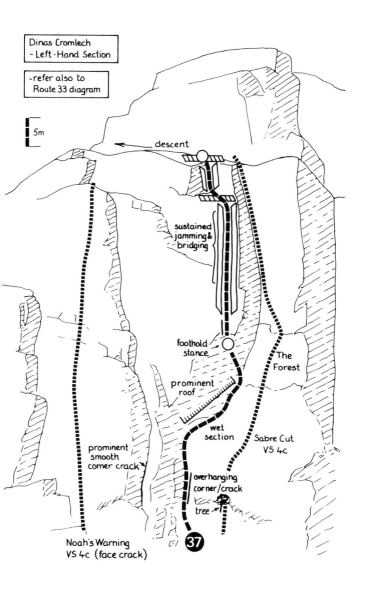

Dinas Cromlech
– Left-Hand Section

–refer also to
Route 33 diagram

5m

descent

sustained
jamming &
bridging

foothold
stance

The Forest

prominent
roof

prominent
smooth
corner crack

wet
section

Sabre Cut
VS 4c

overhanging
corner/crack

tree

Noah's Warning
VS 4c (face crack)

37

# 38: THE CRACKS/SLOW LEDGE (S+) 150m

**Summary:** A great adventure up the Nose and Upper West Wing of Dinas Mot, finest of the Pass crags. Full of intrigue and uncertainty. Direct variants available for scoffing experts. Only the first pitch is poorly protected. The Cracks section is illustrated in detail on Route 39 diagram.

**First Ascent:** The Cracks – B. L. Bathurst and H. C. H. Bathurst, Easter 1930; Slow Ledge – J. M. Edwards and J. Gask, March 1934.

**Best Conditions:** The Nose and West Wing face north at 400m, remaining greasy throughout much of the winter. The lower section is badly affected by drainage from an overlap above the first stance. This rarely dries completely. Slow Ledge is lichenous through lack of traffic – good friction when dry, but exceptionally slippery when wet.

**Approach:** From the lay-by at Pont y Gromlech, as for Route 39.

**Starting Point:** At the lower left side of the Nose, as for Route 39.

**Descent:** (1) When completing only The Cracks section, descend Western Gully from the top of the Nose as for Route 39.

(2) From the top of Slow Ledge, trend left up heather ledges towards the shoulder and descend as for Route 41.

Dinas Mot is the best crag in the Pass. Fascinating contrasts exist between protectionless slabs and safe cracks on the Nose, and between delicate walls and energetic overhangs on the Wings. This intriguing collection of buttresses has the capacity to enthral and entertain long after sunnier cliffs on the north side have lost their superficial appeal.

Most routes on the Nose have three parts: a devious entry; a delicate and poorly protected middle section; and a strenuous finish up the cracked head wall. The Cracks dispenses with the first, compresses the second, and expands the third. Unfortunately, the crack pitches narrowly fail to reach the top. A baffling mantelshelf makes up the shortfall. Athletes surmount it with a Western Roll (maximum of three attempts), while those of more slothful disposition craftily seek out the arête finish.

Slow Ledge shares characteristics with harder climbs of the Wings: an improbable line, lots of overhangs, plenty of exposure. The situation at the Slow Ledge belay is as serious as any on the cliff – and never more so when the leader's feet skid from lichenous holds on the crucial exit.

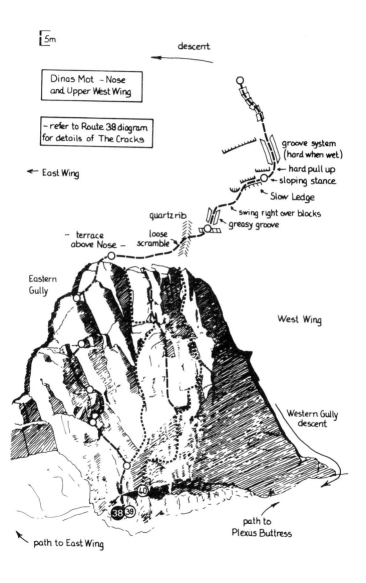

5m

Dinas Mot – Nose
and Upper West Wing

– refer to Route 39 diagram
for details of The Cracks

descent

← East Wing

groove system
(hard when wet)

← hard pull up
← sloping stance
Slow Ledge

swing right over blocks
greasy groove

quartz rib

loose
scramble

– terrace
above Nose –

West Wing

Eastern
Gully

Western Gully
descent

path to
Plexus Buttress

38 39 40

↙ path to East Wing

# 39: DIRECT ROUTE (VS) 75m

**Summary:** A compelling climb in every respect. The finest *VS* in the Pass and one of the very best in Wales. Includes both delicate and strenuous climbing – all on perfect rock. Spaced protection on the groove pitch adds to the experience.

**First Ascent:** C. F. Kirkus and J. B. Dodd, June 1930.

**Best Conditions:** North facing at 400m. Both groove and upper crack are affected by drainage streaks for several days after bad weather.

**Approach:** From the lay-by at Pont y Gromlech. Cross boggy ground, and ascend directly up boulder slopes to the foot of the Nose. Refer to Llanberis Area map. GR.627 563. 20mins.

**Starting Point:** At the lower left side of the Nose, where a slim groove cuts through its undercut base.

**Descent:** Via Western Gully, a clean fissure between the Nose and West Wing (worth roping up, at least for your first descent). The final few metres drop away alarmingly to the scree; look out for a devious rightward traverse (looking in) across wet shelves.

*VS* leaders come of age on the shallow groove pitch of the Direct. Do you know how it feels to make irreversible *4b* moves six, seven or eight metres above the last runner? It feels good. So good in fact that you will keep coming back for more. Lorraine, West Rib, Diagonal: lonely leads worth half a dozen well-protected test-pieces opposite.

The Hand Traverse asks for a different kind of commitment. No shortage of protection here, but the gutsy get-up-and-go technique sufficient for most hand traverses will not work on this inclined flake. A polished foot smear counterbalances an optimistic stretch towards hidden holds.

A returning ledge ends abruptly below the final corner – the first few metres of which are utterly holdless. Colin Kirkus suggested that a ladder would 'make the final crack suitable for other than a few rocks gymnasts'. Your second's shoulder would make a good substitute, except that he stands clutching the belay flake several metres away and refuses to move. Nothing for it then but to jig up the side walls, plant a jam in the bottom of the crack, and finish up the flake like a monkey up a stick. The *5b* technical grade says it all.

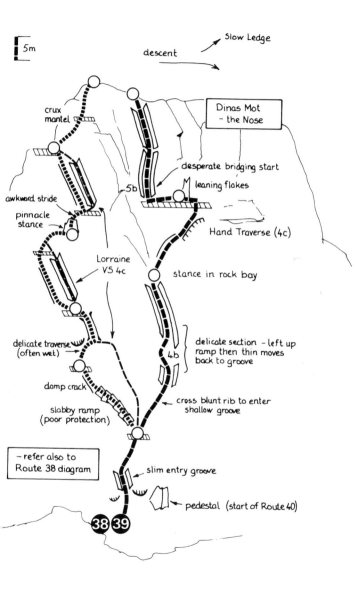

5m

Slow Ledge

descent

crux
mantel

Dinas Mot
– the Nose

desperate bridging start

leaning flakes

awkward stride

5b

pinnacle
stance

Hand Traverse (4c)

Lorraine
VS 4c

stance in rock bay

delicate traverse
(often wet)

delicate section – left up
ramp then thin moves
back to groove

damp crack

4b

slabby ramp
(poor protection)

cross blunt rib to enter
shallow groove

– refer also to
Route 38 diagram

slim entry groove

pedestal (start of Route 40)

38 39

# 40: DIAGONAL (HVS) & SUPERDIRECT (E1) 80m

**Summary:** Bold climbing of great delicacy up the front of the Nose. A devious entry establishes both routes in a commanding position in the centre of the face: Diagonal shirks the main challenge and stumbles upon an unprotected mantelshelf; the Superdirect scrapes together not only a definite line, but also the wherewithal to protect it. Neither route escapes the strenuous cracks of the head wall.

**First Ascent:** Diagonal – A. Birtwistle and G. F. Parkinson, August 1938; Superdirect – R. Evans and H. Pasquill, July 1974.

**Best Conditions:** North facing at 400m. This part of the Nose is spared the drainage problems of The Cracks and the Direct. Nevertheless, climbing of this delicacy on a shady crag is best approached on a warm afternoon without a hint of dampness.

**Approach:** From the lay-by at Pont y Gromlech, as for Route 39.

**Starting Point:** At the lower left side of the Nose, on a pedestal a few metres right of the slim entry groove of the Direct (Route 39).

**Descent:** Down Western Gully as for Route 39.

An era of bold climbing in the thirties reached its zenith with Birtwistle's ascent of Diagonal, climbed by mistake during an attempt on Kirkus's West Rib. It was not repeated for ten years.

The diagonal line, which begins meekly enough as a roller-coaster traverse, soon poses this dilemma: enter the V-chimney via a safe but hard traverse from the Nut Slot; or gain it directly with less difficulty but no protection.

A stance above the chimney provides safe anchorage among a hostile sea of slabs. No one wants to leave. It falls to the least patient partner to quit the ledge and follow a sloping crease towards a shallow groove with few holds and no protection. A handhold on the right seems larger than the others. This is the mantelshelf, and there is no going back.

The Superdirect dodges left from the Nut Slot to discover a slender fault in the seemingly bald face. A final foot-smearing reach wins a rest at a hollow flake, and an easier continuation crack. The top pitch seeks out an equally improbable line. It overhangs viciously and somehow you must find a way to bridge the angle and fix runners without losing momentum. As a pitch in itself it could hold its own at Millstone. No higher praise.

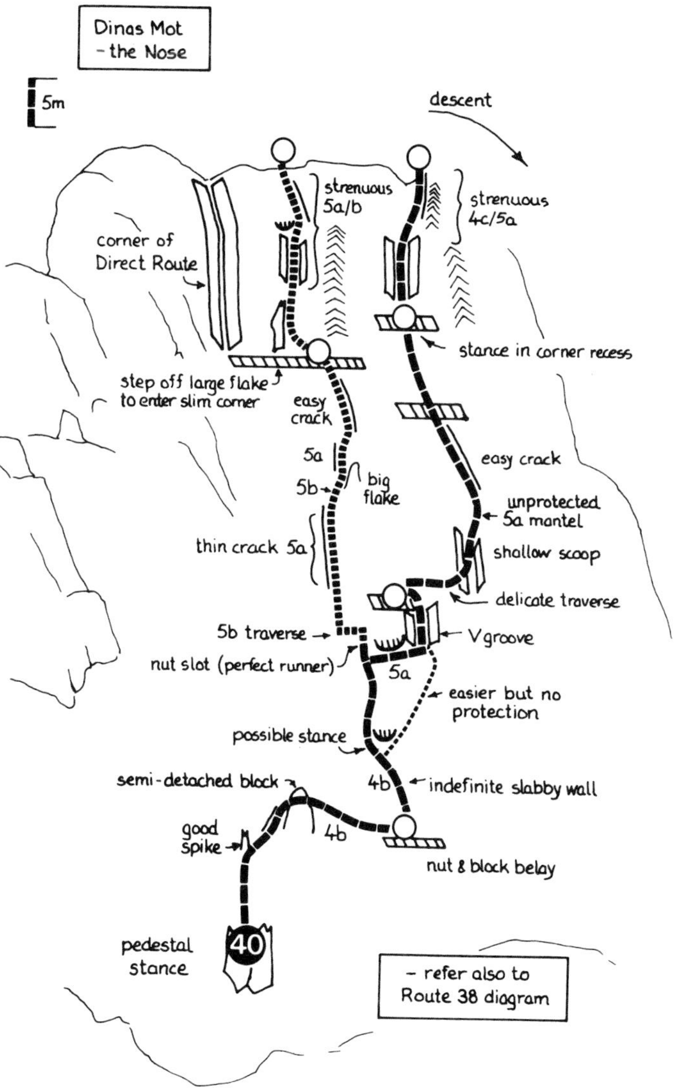

Dinas Mot
– the Nose

5m

descent

strenuous
5a/b

strenuous
4c/5a

corner of
Direct Route

stance in corner recess

step off large flake
to enter slim corner

easy
crack

easy crack

5a

5b

big
flake

unprotected
5a mantel

thin crack 5a

shallow scoop

delicate traverse

5b traverse →

V groove

nut slot (perfect runner)

5a

easier but no
protection

possible stance

semi-detached block →

4b → indefinite slabby wall

good
spike

4b

nut & block belay

pedestal
stance

40

– refer also to
Route 38 diagram

# 41: THE MOLE/GOLLUM (HVS) 110m

**Summary:** An earthy sort of climb, aimlessly wandering through the eaves of the East Wing. Adequate protection; although a leader, or second, climbing carelessly across the diagonal slab risks a pendulum into nowhere. The rock is beautifully brown when dry, biologically green when wet.

**First Ascent:** Mole – J. Brown and E. D. G. Langmuir, April 1961; Gollum – B. C. Webb, A. Harris and V. Cowley, March 1964.

**Best Conditions:** The wing faces north-east at 450m and rarely dries completely. Worth waiting for, because the rough textured rock gives excellent friction when dry.

**Approach:** From the lay-by at Pont y Gromlech to the foot of the Nose, as for Route 39. Ascend scree and boulder slopes up to the left until below the East Wing. Refer to Llanberis Area map. GR.628 563. 25mins.

**Starting Point:** On a grass-topped promontory above the boulder slope. Confirm position by identifying the shallow groove, tree stance and grass terrace.

**Descent:** Ascend heather ledges towards the top of the shoulder. Traverse left into the top of a gully (which defines the left side of the East Wing). Do not descend the gully but cross it and continue left, descending slightly (some scrambling), to enter a boulder-filled canyon. Descend this to scree slopes below the East Wing.

Upward views of the East wing are not encouraging. This perspective hides slabs and gangways, while emphasising overhangs – a deception which helps contain queues to reasonable proportions.

Mole creeps in from high up on the left, while Gollum makes its superior entry over a bulge. Technically, this proves to be as difficult as anything else on the route but, thanks to the nearness of the promontory, seems no more serious than a gritstone boulder problem.

Nothing doing above the tree stance, so stroll across the terrace to see what else is on offer. The obvious slanting slab of Gollum looks promising, but not the overhang which tops it. Mole's solution to the barrier has more subtlety: out left to avoid the first roof, then back right across undercut slabs to avoid the second. Incidentally, if you can beat a breathless Gollum to the next stance you get first crack at its precious exit pitch.

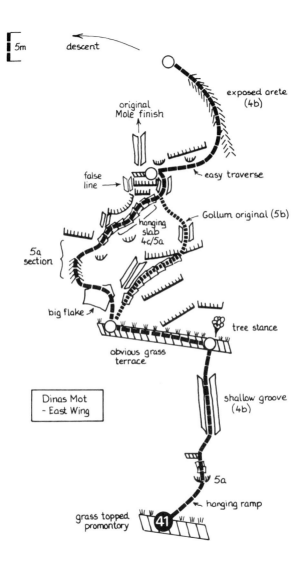

5m

descent

exposed arete
(4b)

original
Mole finish

false
line

easy traverse

Gollum original (5b)

hanging
slab
4c/5a

5a
section

big flake

tree stance

obvious grass
terrace

Dinas Mot
- East Wing

shallow groove
(4b)

5a

hanging ramp

grass topped
promontory

41

# 42: PLEXUS (HVS) 135m

**Summary:** A technically absorbing limb in a huge setting. Plexus Buttress remains private, despite three excellent routes and the proximity of the Llanberis Pass. Rock texture and type of holds are reminiscent of gritstone. Spaced protection.

**First Ascent:** B. Ingle and P. Crew, October 1962.

**Best Conditions:** North-west facing at an altitude of 450m. Requires several fine days to dry out after wet weather. The lichenous rock becomes extremely slippery when wet, but gives superb friction when dry.

**Approach:** As for Route 39 to below the Nose. Cross the ladder stile on the right, and continue traversing below the West Wing. Enter the first major recess in the cliff barrier, and scramble up rightwards to a terrace below the isolated Plexus Buttress. Refer to Llanberis area map. GR.626 563. 25mins.

**Starting Point:** At the right end of a shattered lower wall, where a small groove leads up to the right end of a ledge.

**Descent:** (1) Gain the heather shoulder above the main part of the crag and descend as for Route 41 (assuming rucksacks have been left below the Nose).

(2) Descend Jammed Boulder Gully (*D*), with considerable difficulty. (This gully defines the left side of the recess entered during the approach.)

Plexus Buttress does not fully reveal itself during a brief flirtation with Plexus, but only after a long-running affair which also encompasses Nexus and Ten Degrees North. It seems a little unfair to elevate just one of these climbs to 'classic' status when the truth is that warm recollection of one ascent automatically ignites into fiery anticipation of the next.

The first of several 'moments' on Plexus arrives while attempting to occupy an undercut slab on the first main pitch. Two possible strategies suggest themselves. The first is to step right, on an inadequate crease, and then grovel for a finger flake. The second, is to pull up into a groove on the left, and then swing right using a good hold on the rib. (Clue: for God's sake go left!)

The top crux, a nominal *5b* reach through overhangs, unfairly discriminates against climbers of less than average height. A peg for aid puts them on an equal footing.

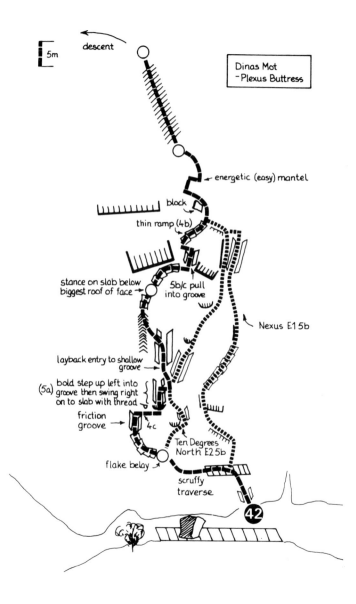

5m

descent

Dinas Mot
- Plexus Buttress

energetic (easy) mantel

block

thin ramp (4b)

stance on slab below
biggest roof of face

5b/c pull
into groove

Nexus E1 5b

layback entry to shallow
groove

(5a) bold step up left into
groove then swing right
on to slab with thread

friction
groove

4c

Ten Degrees
North E2 5b

flake belay

scruffy
traverse

42

# 43: MAIN WALL (S+) 145m

**Summary:** An audacious mountaineering route up the most imposing cliff in the Pass. Intricate route
finding, indifferent protection, unremitting exposure. The most sought
after of Welsh *Severes*. Double
ropes recommended.

**First Ascent:** P. L. Roberts and J.
K. Cooke, May 1937.

**Best Conditions:** North-east facing at 600m. Most of the difficult
climbing takes place on open walls
which, in summer at least, will dry
within a day or so of rain. Rarely in
condition from November to March.
Start early to catch a few hours of
morning sunlight.

**Approach:** As for Route 44.

**Starting Point:** Not easy to identify.
Scramble up a rib, and traverse left
to belay at the right end of a ledge.
About 10m above and to the right is
a conspicuous triangular overhang:
the first pitch of 12m follows a
slanting groove steeply up left to
gain a ledge at the same level as
this overhang before traversing left
to a huge spike belay.

**Descent:** Scramble upwards then
contour left into upper Cwm Glas.
Either continue up Clogwyn y
Ddysgl (Route 46) or return to lower
Cwm Glas by descending the path
well to the east of Cyrn Las.

Clumsy in boots, gravity clutching at your rucksack straps, you
kick from beneath the pitch two overhang, and make a bid for the
pulpit stance. Gone are the preoccupations with style and
measured execution; this is the real thing, the epitome of mountain
rock climbs.

A delicate ramp – the technical crux in stiff boots – slants
across the wall towards a dripping corner. The corner: was this
glaringly obvious line the objective of the pioneers? If so then they
must have been bitterly disappointed – Subsidiary Groove struggles to climb it at *E1*! Nothing for it but to go back left to a stance
on the arête. Here pegs driven unconvincingly into the floor do little
to calm the waves of exposure now breaking over the cliff.

A third diagonal returns to the sinister corner again, but this time
the escape is more involved. It includes a loose crack, an awkward
pull into a niche, and an exit into a position of extreme exposure on
the arête. This is the Main Wall of repute: big, intricate, and
unforgiving. The final hanging slab, elegantly poised above Great
Gully, brings more immediate rewards.

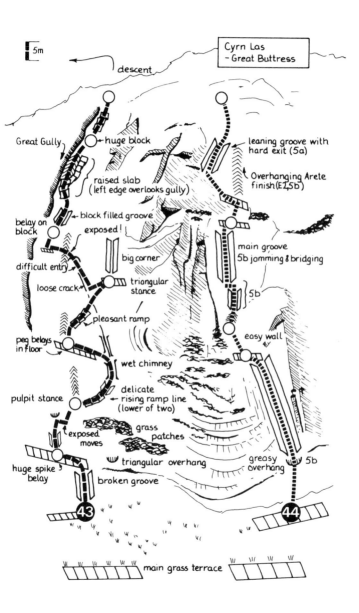

**Cyrn Las – Great Buttress**

5m

descent

Great Gully

huge block

raised slab
(left edge overlooks gully)

leaning groove with
hard exit (5a)

Overhanging Arete
finish (E1,5b)

belay on
block

block filled groove

exposed!

big corner

main groove
5b jamming & bridging

difficult entry

loose crack

triangular
stance

5b

pleasant ramp

peg belays
in floor

easy wall

wet chimney

pulpit stance

delicate
rising ramp line
(lower of two)

grass
patches

exposed
moves

huge spike
belay

triangular overhang

broken groove

greasy
overhang    5b

**43**

**44**

main grass terrace

# 44: THE GROOVES (E1) 115m

**Summary:** Direct and uncompromising, this coveted route ranks alongside the great Cloggy *Extremes* for position and atmosphere. Strenuous jamming and bridging throughout. Good protection. Illustrated on Route 43 diagram.

**First Ascent:** J. Brown, D. Cowan and E. Price, September 1953.

**Best Conditions:** The crag faces north-east at an altitude of 600m, and as such remains inhospitable throughout the winter months. Even in summer the grooves take several days to dry out after rain.

**Approach:** From the Llanberis Pass (parking in lay-bys). Cross the river and its tributary at Blaen y Nant (GR.623 570). Ascend steep grass slopes into lower Cwm Glas. Continue by the west bank of the stream for a little way then cross to approach the left side of the cliff barrier. The Great Buttress itself stands on a plinth of broken slabs. Avoid these by scrambling diagonally from the left to a grassy terrace. Refer to Llanberis Area map. GR.615 560. 45mins.

**Starting Point:** Below an overhang which undercuts the initial groove. Refer to Route 43 diagram for location.

**Descent:** Well to the left of the cliff, as for Route 43.

Encounters with Cyrn Las are momentuous affairs. Denied an opportunity for gradual progression through the grades, the familiarisation process must be hurried along on the day.

The first overhang, poised above ugly splinters, is not very nice. Some attempts founder even at this early stage, cast back from the dripping bulge by a tide of uncertainty. What does lie beyond? Chances of success improve in direct proportion to increasing curiosity, so better say nothing.

This strategy does not work on the crucial middle pitch. Here some other mechanism bridges the body precariously up that open groove to nowhere. From its top a blind swing gains the main groove. The new problem proves to be an unrelenting finger-to-fist jamming pitch. Perfect protection rewards commitment.

Huge spikes clutter the entry to the final groove. No complaints, except to suggest that a more thoughtful distributor would have held back a couple for the exit. As it is, the supplied finger holds, stock-in-trade lower down the climb, are meagre support for tired arms. The climb that began with a whimper ends with a scream.

# 45: PARSLEY FERN GULLY (I or II) 300m

**Summary:** A reliable introduction to winter climbing although, by following an open couloir, it lacks the atmosphere of a true gully. Extremely popular. Some stances can be secured by rock anchors, otherwise by deadmen or buried axes. Not illustrated – refer to Llanberis Area map for location.

**First Ascent:** Not known.

**Best Conditions:** Faces north-east at an altitude of 800–1000m. Old snow frozen by a night of penetrating frost produces the best conditions. February and early March are generally the best months, although in some years it can attain climbable condition at any time from November to early May.

**Approach:** Enter lower Cwm Glas as for Route 44, then ascend into the upper cwm by rocky slopes well to the left of Cyrn Las. The gully is now obvious as a long, uninterrupted strip of snow on the right of the cwm head wall. This approach to upper Cwm Glas can be extremely tedious. In suitable conditions – after several days of subzero temperatures – the stream course left of Cyrn Las provides an excellent diversion on grade *III* ice. GR.613 555. 1hr 15mins.

**Starting Point:** At the foot of the gully.

**Descent:** (1) Return to Pen y Pass via Route 47 or one of its emergency descents.
(2) Return to upper Cwm Glas via slopes a few hundred metres to the right of the gully (not recommended for inexperienced parties).

Under normal conditions the gully consists almost entirely of a snow couloir. Usually a small ice pitch develops in the Narrows at about half height, but this could be obscured by deep snow. Direct exits will steepen at a line of cornices at the rim. These are usually small, but if necessary can be flanked to right or left. The Left Hand finish breaks off from below the Narrows, to give an interesting finish on steeper ice and snow.

You will need to be especially cautious when assessing conditions, and deciding how much of the route can be safely climbed unroped. It is usual to solo up the easy lower part to a rock belay below the narrow middle section, but this will depend on conditions. When stripped of snow, or after a prolonged frost without snowfall, the route may consist wholly of a ribbon of water-ice. In these circumstances the route can be quite difficult and time consuming.

# 46: GAMBIT CLIMB (VD+) 100m

**Summary:** Varied climbing up a series of strenuous cracks on a remote mountain crag. The rock is generally excellent, marred only by a loose band at mid-height. Protection available for major difficulties.

**First Ascent:** J. M. A. Thomson, H. O. Jones and K. J. P. Orton, September 1910.

**Best Conditions:** Faces northwest at 750m. Rarely in condition from November to March. However, comparative lack of drainage means that in high summer the route will dry quickly after rain. Idyllic in the late afternoon sun.

**Approach:** As for Route 44 to lower Cwm Glas. Ascend well to the left of Cyrn Las to enter upper Cwm Glas. Alternatively, approach via Main Wall (Route 43). Refer to Llanberis area map. GR.616 555. 1hr 15mins.

**Starting Point:** Refer to crag diagram and following text.

**Descent:** (1) Ascend the easy upper part of Clogwyn y Person Arête to a junction with Route 47.

(2) Turn left to descend the awkward lower section of the arête (complex route finding). Do not descend the final step into the notch behind the Parson's Nose, but scramble down the wall to its right (looking in) to enter the lower section of Western Gully.

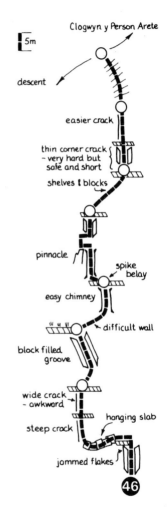

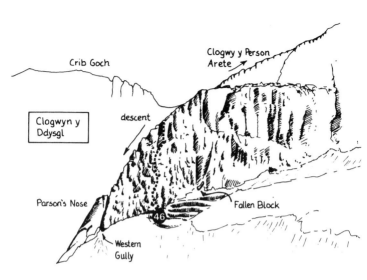

Crib Goch

Clogwy y Person Arete

Clogwyn y Ddysgl

descent

Parson's Nose

Fallen Block

46

Western Gully

Clogwyn y Ddysgl is too remote, and too often shrouded in mist, ever to become popular. It is a crag full of secrets. Here you can discover unclimbed rock that on a valley crag would have been climbed and become polished many decades ago. The most rewarding area for investigation will be found midway between Western Gully and the Fallen Block. Here a terraced wall of pumice-like rock guards the main face. Easy scrambling up its left side leads to a short corner with two jammed flakes. A block of pumice rock leans against the wall to provide a convenient thread belay. This looks promising! Hard luck – others have been this way before. You've found The Gambit.

Apart from a few exceptions the routes here lack line and continuity. On any other mountain crag this would be unacceptable, but here the individual pitches are technically so engrossing that overall direction seems unimportant. The Gambit incorporates three unrelated pitches of outstanding merit: an entry slab sandwiched between two strenuous cracks; a well-positioned and improbably steep upper chimney; and a desperately hard (but short and safe) final corner crack.

# Snowdon Area

Snowdon is a fascinating mountain. Six major ridges extend from its summit, each supporting a popular walk. When linked together, the western ridges, known as the Snowdon Horseshoe, produce a ridge traverse of outstanding quality.

From the climbing point of view, only one of the corresponding six cwms is barren, although two more lack popular appeal and are unable to nominate a route for this selection. That leaves us with the pastoral north-western Cwm Brwynog, which terminates abruptly in the magnificent cliff of Clogwyn Du'r Arddu, and the huge western cwm circled by the Horseshoe, which accommodates Lliwedd and Clogwyn y Garnedd. Cwm Glas, the third remaining cwm, is decribed within the Llanberis Pass section.

The majority of routes in this section have been drawn from the impressive north-facing walls of Clogwyn Du'r Arddu. And rightly so: 'Cloggy' is not only the finest cliff in North Wales, but is at the heart of all British rock climbing. Lliwedd, itself at the forefront of the sport during the first decade of the twentieth century, now languishes in almost total neglect. Climbers have grown too impatient for these rambling climbs, and yet their scale and atmosphere surpass any other in this book.

It is no surprise that the most reliable winter climbing in Wales is to be found on the north face of Snowdon itself. Mid-grade mountaineers have made sunless Clogwyn y Garnedd their grim winter playground.

**Approaches:** Most routes described in this section are approached either from Llanberis (for Clogwyn Du'r Arddu) or Pen y Pass (for Lliwedd & Clogwyn y Garnedd) on the A4086. A bus route serves Llanberis and Nant Peris (via Caernarfon). In summer the Sherpa bus service links Nant Peris, via Pen y Pass, to Pen y Gwryd (connections to Capel Curig and Beddgelert).

**Accommodation:** *Camping*: As for Llanberis Area plus Llyn Gwynant, 4km south of Pen y Gwryd near A498 (GR.648 525).
*High camps/bivouacs*: Llyn Llydaw (for Lliwedd) and Llyn Du'r Arddu (for Clogwyn Du'r Arddu).
*Youth Hostels*: Llanberis, Pen y Pass and Bryn Gwynant.
Other accommodation and services as for Llanberis Area.

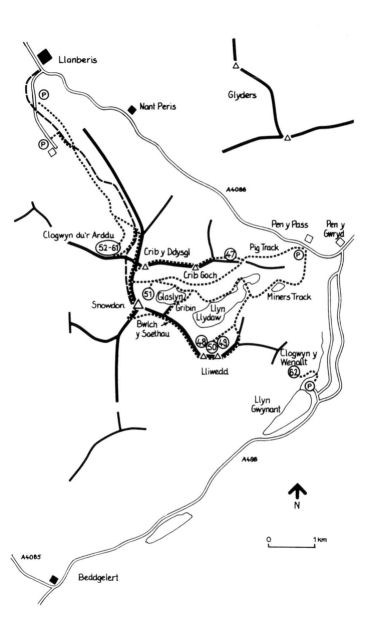

*Nearing the top of Shrike (Route 53), Clogwyn Du'r Arddu.*

*The big pitch on White Slab (Route 60), Clogwyn Du'r Arddu. The climber above has just succeeded in lassoing the spike and is about to pendulum across the slab.*

# 47: SNOWDON HORSESHOE (E or I/II) 12km

**Summary:** The classic circuit of Snowdon and the most popular ridge traverse in Britain. Summer or winter it gives a long but extremely satisfying day. Serious accidents occur each year on Crib Goch, often as a consequence of under-estimating weather and ground conditions. Axe, crampons and rope are essential equipment in winter.

**Best Conditions:** Any calm day from spring to autumn for a 'summer' traverse (Crib Goch is extremely exposed to strong winds). Route finding is intricate rather than vague, so low cloud need not be a problem. Under (rare) ideal winter conditions of deep, consolidated snow the traverse has no equal in Welsh mountaineering. Powder snow, hoar frost and ice are more typical. In these conditions the route can be quite difficult and insecure.

**Starting Point:** At Pen y Pass car-park (GR.647 556); fee payable at weekends and during holiday periods (often full after 9.00am). Alternatively, park at Pen y Gwryd (GR.660 558) and walk up to Pen y Pass – 20mins.

**Emergency Descents:** Refer also to Snowdon Area map.
  (1)  Bwlch Coch via Cwm Glas to Llanberis Pass.
  (2) Crib y Ddysgl via Llanberis Path to Llanberis.
  (3) Crib y Ddysgl via Pig Track/Miners Track (exit from Zig-Zags sometimes corniced) to Pen y Pass.
  (4) Snowdon Summit via South Ridge (narrow ridge in early stages) to Nant Gwynant.
  (5) Bwlch y Saethau via Watkin Path to Nant Gwynant.
  (6) Bwlch y Saethau via Gribin (rock scrambling) to Pen y Pass.

Most choose to traverse the Horseshoe in an anticlockwise direction, thereby tackling the difficult section while still fresh. Besides, those attempting the reverse tour risk being cast back by a wave of conformists.

Horseshoeists quit the Pig Track at Bwlch y Moch (with its surprise view of Lliwedd) for the barren East Ridge. An initial rock barrier may cause problems, but there is an easier way up to the left if you can find it. Thereafter, the best line follows the crest more or less directly, although in winter the snow runnels to right and left make tempting alternatives.

Crib Goch is the highlight of the day. A narrow section arrives first, its toothed crest a convenient handrail (although extrovert or insured scramblers will stand upright and balance across unaided). These antics apart, the greatest difficulties arise when

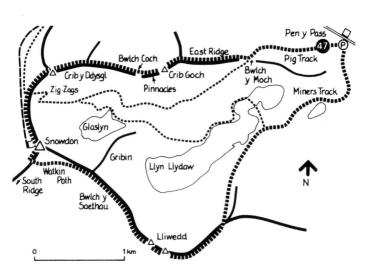

traversing the Pinnacles. Flanking routes on the left encounter more problems than they solve; the best line weaves through just a few metres below their summits. Take extra care in winter when ice or powder snow obscures the holds.

Bwlch Coch brings a rare moment of relaxation before scrambling resumes on Crib y Ddysgl. Once again the best summer line stays close to the crest, while in winter it may be best to quit the ridge after a few hundred metres for snow ramps on its northern flank. The circuit from Crib y Ddysgl to Snowdon summit presents no difficulties.

Direct descents from Snowdon Summit to Bwlch y Saethau are a mistake. Instead, follow the South Ridge for two hundred metres to a marker post, and then descend diagonally across broken slopes (this is the Watkin Path). Note that when iced, it may be impossible to arrest a slide here with an ice axe.

At the end of a long day the prospect of Lliwedd from Bwlch y Saethau can be psychologically devastating. In reality its curving armchair ridges present few real difficulties while providing breathtaking views of its north-east face. After the hustle and bustle of Snowdon, this shapely satellite peak restores a proper sense of dignity and concludes the traverse in style.

# 48: SLANTING BUTTRESS (D) 225m

**Summary:** Traditional mountain rock climbing in imposing surroundings. Interesting and varied without being excessively difficult.

**First Ascent:** G. D. Abraham and A. P. Abraham, April 1904.

**Best Conditions:** Faces north-east at 750m. Sustains limited drainage, and in summer should dry within a day or so of rain. Untypically positive footholds make this the best wet-weather climb on the mountain.

**Approach:** From Pen y Pass. Refer to Route 47 for details. Follow the Miners Track to Llyn Llydaw, from where the reclining bulk of Lliwedd is clearly visible. Turn left along the shore and follow the obvious rising track. The track steepens. After about 100m, break off right along a narrow path, and contour the hillside to scree below the cliffs. Refer to Snowdon Area map. GR.623 535. 1hr.

**Starting Point:** At the lower left end of the rightmost of two obvious quartz stripes (refer to crag drawing).

**Descent:** (1) Turn right and descend to Bwlch y Saethau. Descend the Gribin to Glaslyn and return to Pen y Pass via the Miners Track. Refer to Route 47 map.
(2) Turn left and ascend to the summit. Descend as for Route 49.

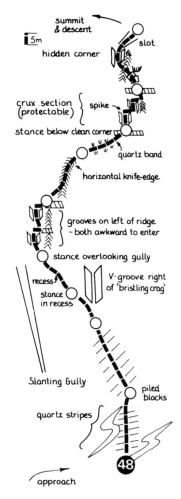

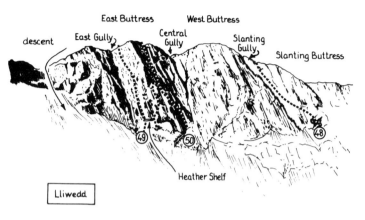

East Buttress  West Buttress

descent  East Gully  Central Gully  Slanting Gully  Slanting Buttress

Heather Shelf

Lliwedd

Lliwedd became a forcing ground for Welsh climbing during the early years of the twentieth century. Although its heyday lasted only a decade, it built in that short time a reputation powerful enough to maintain a dwindling clientele for a further thirty years. Nowadays, the majority of North Wales regulars have not even seen Lliwedd, let alone set foot on it. In the years before final neglect it became fashionable to pour scorn on the place, but none who have actually climbed here will deny Lliwedd the respect it deserves.

Slanting Buttress proves to be the most straightforward route on the `cliff (although a few terrifying scrambles purport to be technically easier). As such, it makes an ideal introduction to the cliff for a comparatively inexperienced party, or if conditions are less than perfect. After an uninspiring start on the splayed buttress foot it veers towards a narrower ridge overlooking Slanting Gully. With increasing interest it then follows a series of grooves and ramps until the ridge narrows again and falls back as a knife-edge. The upper wall rises above, climbed by a relatively safe but intimidating corner pitch. A surprise exit adds one final twist to the saga.

## 49: HORNED CRAG (VD+) 260m

**Summary:** A mountaineering route of character and interest. Awesome difficulties await those who fail to solve the route finding riddles. Good protection available when it matters most.

**First Ascent:** J. M. A. Thomson and O. Eckenstein, September 1905.

**Best Conditions:** The cliff faces north-east at an altitude of 750m. Rarely is it in good condition between October and April. During warm or windy weather in summer it should dry within two days of rain. Difficulties increase dramatically if the sloping holds are at all damp.

**Approach:** From Pen y Pass as for Route 48. Refer to Snowdon Area map. GR.625 533. 1hr.

**Starting Point:** At a bollard on the left side of Heather Shelf, gained by a scramble from the left. Refer to Route 48 crag drawing.

**Descent:** (1) Descend the summit ridge leftwards, and return to Llyn Llydaw as for Route 47.
(2) Descend the short gully left of Far East Buttress, and return over scree to the foot of the climb. Refer to Route 48 crag drawing.

While recovering at the shore of Llyn Llydaw, trace the line of Horned Crag up the East Buttress. See how the sun warms the rocks with its golden glow? How easy and inviting it looks!

Form and sunlight disappear on close approach. The buttress falls back in a shapeless pile of blocks and heather ledges. Only the pale scars of clumsy passage betray the devious line.

The trail goes cold at half height where footmark evidence scatters in all directions. Somewhere above should be a 'Horned Crag', but attempts to isolate it topographically from the jumbled mass of other crags would be as futile as describing faces in a fire.

A common mistake is to dismiss as 'impossible', when it is merely improbable, the crack which exits a V-shaped recess. Face reality: make it safe and then get on with it. The cracked slab above tests your resolve a second time. A moment before a slip seems inevitable the route dodges left to ledges and twin pillars – the Horns!

The right hand pillar and quartz-veined wall complete the Horned Crag episode; now only easy grooves and scrambling remain. Meanwhile, those of lesser faith are still lurching about somewhere far below, confined to their epic destiny.

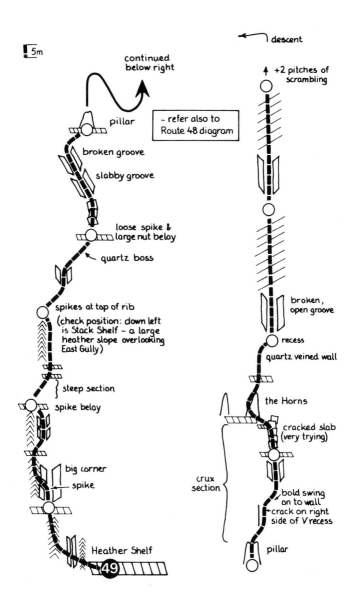

5m

descent

continued below right

+2 pitches of scrambling

pillar

- refer also to Route 48 diagram

broken groove

slabby groove

loose spike & large nut belay

quartz boss

broken, open groove

spikes at top of rib
(check position: down left is Stack Shelf – a large heather slope overlooking East Gully)

recess

quartz veined wall

the Horns

steep section

spike belay

cracked slab (very trying)

big corner

spike

crux section

bold swing on to wall

crack on right side of V recess

Heather Shelf

49

pillar

# 50: ROUTE II/RED WALL (S) 300m

**Summary:** A serious and committing climb up the biggest cliff in Wales. Good judgement, confidence, and perfect conditions, will compensate for suspect belays and inadequate protection.

**First Ascent:** Route II – J. M. A. Thomson and O. Eckenstein, April 1903; Red Wall (by the Avalanche start) – J. M. A. Thomson and E. S. Reynolds, September 1907; Longland's Continuation – J. L. Longland and party, Easter 1929.

**Best Conditions:** As for Route 49.

**Approach:** From Pen y Pass as for Route 48. Refer to Snowdon Area map. GR.625 533. 1hr.

**Starting Point:** At the upper right end of a 50m quartz stripe which wriggles through the lowest rocks of East Buttress and points to the start of Shallow Gully.

**Descent:** As for Route 49.

Progress on Lliwedd is measured not by move but by pitch. This route has about fourteen of them, but who's counting? The first two are concerned only with escaping the funnel of Shallow Gully to reach the Quartz Babe. Lliwedd experts (not many of those about) will reach the Babe directly by climbing The Sword (*VS*) up the rib left of the normal start.

Allocating names to rock features does little to ease Lliwedd's chronic route finding problems. However, it does lend an air of authority to the guide writer's prose and no doubt gave amusement to the pioneers. And so it is that two pitches later you will find yourself heaving up on the spontaneously named Thank God Holds – reputedly the first of many in climbing history.

All this and more leads to the Great Terrace which, had you been swayed by popular opinion, you would have gained by taking the rattling trail up ugly but widely publicised Avalanche Route – paradoxically the busiest climb on Lliwedd. Either way, the outlook from the terrace is extremely grim. It is bad enough that you must embark on the crucial and totally committing Red Wall without proper belays, but to do so without being able to locate its start with absolute certainty seems quite unfair. Such is Lliwedd.

Once above Red Wall there is no going back as Longland's Continuation, poised above the sweeping walls of the East Buttress, gathers itself together for an appropriately bold finale. Fittingly it emerges within a spit of the summit.

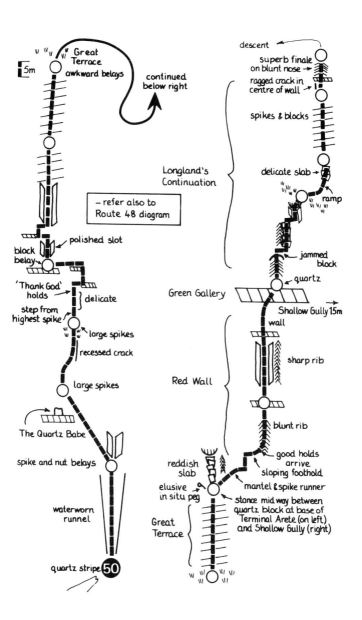

descent

superb finale
on blunt nose →

ragged crack in
centre of wall

spikes & blocks

delicate slab →

Longland's
Continuation

ramp

jammed
block

quartz

Green Gallery

Shallow Gully 15m

wall

sharp rib

Red Wall

blunt rib

good holds
arrive
sloping foothold

reddish
slab

mantel & spike runner

elusive →
in situ peg

stance mid way between
quartz block at base of
Terminal Arete (on left)
and Shallow Gully (right)

Great
Terrace

Great
Terrace
awkward belays

continued
below right

5m

polished slot

block
belay

– refer also to
Route 48 diagram

'Thank God'
holds

delicate

step from
highest spike

large spikes

recessed crack

large spikes

The Quartz Babe

spike and nut belays

waterworn
runnel

quartz stripe **50**

# 51: TRINITY FACE ROUTES (I to III) 200m

**Summary:** A selection of popular snow couloirs and gullies high on the northern flank of Snowdon. The largest concentration of medium grade winter routes in Wales. All are serious undertakings, because of variable weather and conditions and the scarcity of good belays.

**Best Conditions:** North-east facing at 900m. Accumulations of water-ice are minimal and so consolidated snow produces the best conditions. Risk of avalanche or cornice collapse during thaw or after heavy snow. (Refer also to main text.)

**Approach:** From Pen y Pass car-park. Refer to Route 47 for details. Follow the Pig Track across the southern flank of Crib Goch to a promontory overlooking Glaslyn (fine views of Snowdon East Face). Continue for a few hundred metres beyond its junction with the Miners Track before breaking off left (beware of snow covered mine entrances!), to arrive below the Trinity Face at a tiny lake. Refer to

Snowdon Area map. GR.612 547. 1hr 30mins in good conditions.

**Starting Point:** Refer to the crag drawing, which corresponds to a foreshortened view of the face from the usual approach. It is important to locate the start of the routes before approaching too closely, when gross foreshortening will destroy any overall picture of the face. Note especially the start of routes in relation to the spidery Trinity Snowfield.

**Descent:** All climbs finish at the summit of Snowdon or on its north-west ridge:

(1) Descend the ridge to a shallow col and finger stone where the Pig Track Zig-Zags emerge. Descend these to rejoin the approach path at its junction with the Miners Track.

(2) In good conditions it may be convenient to descend a short snow gully right of Cave Gully (grade *I*).

Ideal conditions for the Trinity Face often develop late in the season when old snow, stripped of powder by rain or thaw, freezes hard during a night frost. Few other winter venues, bearing in mind this one straddles the 1000m contour, are capable of withstanding such severe scouring. This explains why a crag as remote as Clogwyn y Garnedd can become so crowded. Some of these gullies frequently attain climbable condition, although in sparse conditions their upper slopes will offer little prospect of belay security.

Trinity Face climbs lack the ferocity of other Welsh gullies and

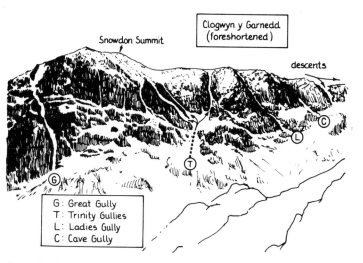

Snowdon Summit

Clogwyn y Garnedd
(foreshortened)

descents

G: Great Gully
T: Trinity Gullies
L: Ladies Gully
C: Cave Gully

ice-falls. Central and Left-Hand Trinity gullies, both grade *I* in good conditions, are especially popular among aspiring winter mountaineers. Towards the end of the season, however, or after low temperatures without snowfall, Central Trinity may consist entirely of a narrow strip of bare ice. In these conditions it can be quite trying.

Right-Hand Trinity shares the common Trinity start before moving right to follow a much more difficult line up steep snow (grade *II/III*). Lean conditions will expose a tricky rock section here.

Great Gully (grade *II* when complete) attracts more attention than it fully deserves, although compared to the Trinities the confined lower section has more of the character of a true gully. Its ridge finish to the summit adds length and alpine flavour.

Although shorter than most routes here, Ladies Gully and Cave Gully are the most memorable (both grade *III* in good conditions, but *IV* otherwise). In Cave Gully the confined runnel and leftward cave exit at half height are especially exciting. Ladies Gully is longer and perhaps the more difficult of the two under borderline conditions. In a good season its steepening runnel and V-groove, again at half height, will give superb climbing on snow-ice.

# 52: THE MOSTEST (E2) 100m

**Summary:** A daunting climb up the exposed front face of Cloggy's Far East Buttress. Difficulties steadily increase to a trying exit from the hanging groove. Good protection. Some doubtful rock.

**First Ascent:** J. Brown (unseconded), April 1957.

**Best Conditions:** North facing at 850m. Rarely in condition outside the period May to September. The hanging groove suffers drainage, and requires several days to dry out after heavy rain.

**Approach:** As for Route 54 to where the Cloggy path breaks off, 1km beyond Halfway House. Continue up the Llanberis Path to where it passes beneath the railway. Follow the railway for a few hundred metres then contour right to arrive at the top of the Far East Buttress (refer to Snowdon Area map). Alternatively approach from the top of the main cliff. Finally descend with care down the Far Eastern Terrace (refer to Route 53 crag drawing). GR.602 554. 1hr 30mins.

**Starting Point:** At a good belay where the terrace fizzles out above an awesome drop.

**Descent:** Return by the approach route; or walk righwards and descend Eastern Terrace, as for Route 53, to the foot of the main cliff.

Climbing on the Far East Buttress is a unique experience. On the main cliff you have an opportunity to study your route beforehand, measure the task, learn from other climbers already at work. Not here. Here you commit yourself on the strength of a clinical route description and a hazy view from across the valley.

The climb begins with a scruffy pitch – supposedly easy but not – of no particular merit. Shrug off the unexpected struggle and apply a steady hand to the first main pitch, the object of which is to gain a foothold, literally, in the bottom of the hanging groove. Now solve a wall of Llithrig-like intricacy and difficulty, daunting enough down below on the 'friendly' East Buttress, but here magnified to *Extreme* proportions. A continuing supply of runners and holds, mostly solid, replenishes the evaporating dribble of confidence.

A semi-hanging stance at the foothold eases physical, not mental, pain. Could this be the most exposed stance on Cloggy? The hanging groove brings protection but no worthwhile rest and delivers you, unprepared, at the crucial exit beneath the overhang. There's no time for second thoughts. Probably just as well.

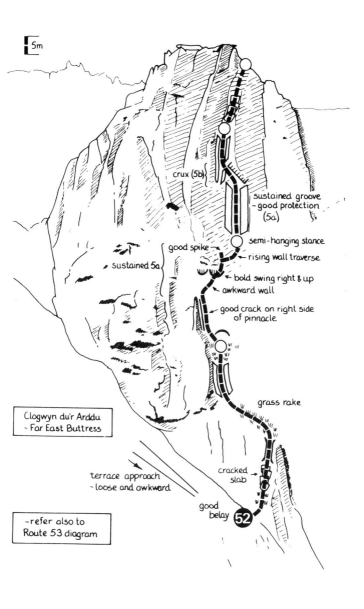

5m

crux (5b)

sustained groove
- good protection
(5a)

semi-hanging stance

good spike

rising wall traverse

sustained 5a

bold swing right & up

awkward wall

good crack on right side
of pinnacle

grass rake

Clogwyn du'r Arddu
- Far East Buttress

terrace approach
- loose and awkward

cracked
slab

good belay  **52**

-refer also to
Route 53 diagram

# 53: SHRIKE (E1) 60m

**Summary:** Magnificent face climbing high on the East Gully Wall of the Pinnacle. Strenuous and exposed. Good protection for the hardest moves, adequate elsewhere.

**First Ascent:** J. Brown, H. Smith and J. Smith, October 1958.

**Best Conditions:** East facing at 850m. Carries almost no drainage, and in summer catches the sun until late morning. Likely to be cold and damp during the period November to March.

**Approach:** (1) Gain the foot of the East Buttress, as for Route 54, and then creep carefully up East Gully almost to where it steepens into a rotten corner chimney. A worrying scramble. 1hr 15mins.
 (2) From Eastern Terrace gain the top of the Pinnacle's East Gully Wall and abseil down the upper chimney of East Gully. A worrying abseil.

**Starting Point:** About 50m right of the East Gully corner, where a pinnacle leans against the wall.

**Descent:** Traverse rightwards into the upper scree filled chute of Eastern Terrace. Descend slabs, ramps, and finally a wet staircase, to grass below the Boulder. Now turn right (facing out) and descend the ramp which slants back beneath the East Buttress (some scrambling).

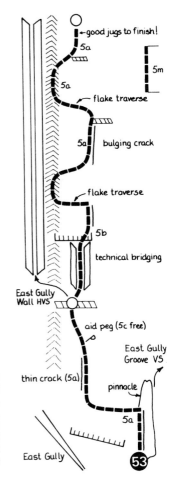

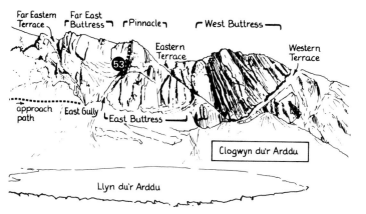

Far Eastern Terrace

Far East Buttress

Pinnacle

West Buttress

Eastern Terrace

Western Terrace

53

approach path

East Gully

East Buttress

Clogwyn du'r Arddu

Llyn du'r Arddu

Shrike is so wrapped up in its remote amphitheatre setting that, to most viewpoints, it reveals no more than a glimpse of itself. But you don't risk your neck scrambling up East Gully simply to 'take a closer look'. You go up there to give it your best.

The first pitch begins up an awkward pinnacle crack but leaves it after just three metres for a traverse above the undercut. Strong, skilful climbers will now climb up to a peg and pass it with a fingery *5c* move. Honest, feeble climbers will struggle merely to reach it and therefore will not hesitate to use it for aid or resting.

Spurn the easier finish of East Gully Wall (*HVS*) and embark instead on the opening bridging sequence of Shrike's main pitch. An overhang guards its upper wall. There's talk of a super-jug over the lip. Can this be true? Place a good nut and find out! A flake traverse beyond hints at rare delights to come. Runners could be better, but who cares? On a wall of this angle there's nothing to hit anyway! Besides, there's good holds and half-rests all the way to the top. Almost.

# 54: LLITHRIG/PINNACLE ARÊTE (E1) 140m

**Summary:** Classic East Buttress face climbing followed by a bold finish up the Pinnacle's towering left edge. Unrelenting verticality and exposure. Good protection for the hardest moves.

**First Ascent:** Llithrig – J. Brown and J. R. Allen, June 1952; Pinnacle Arête – M. Boysen and C. J. Mortlock, June 1962.

**Best Conditions:** North facing at 750m. Most of the hard climbing takes place on open walls which should dry out within a day or so of rain, at least during the period late spring to autumn.

**Approach:** From Llanberis, follow a minor road opposite the Royal Victoria Hotel for about 2km. Small parking place. Ascend a boggy slope to the railway, and follow this to a bridge over the Llanberis Path (alternatively, park after 1km and follow the Llanberis Path throughout). Take the path and fork right about 1km beyond Halfway House, circling high above Llyn Du'r Arddu to arrive below the East Buttress. Refer to Snowdon Area map. GR.602 556. 1hr.

**Starting Point:** On ledges below a left facing chimney-crack. Refer to crag drawing.

**Descent:** Escape rightwards up short walls and terraces. Descend Eastern Terrace as for Route 53.

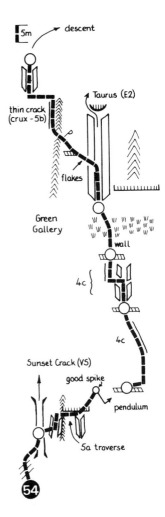

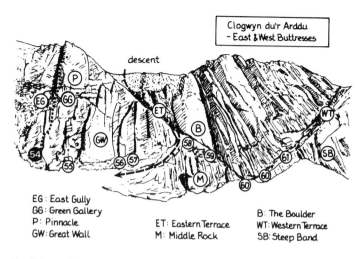

Clogwyn du'r Arddu
– East & West Buttresses

descent

EG : East Gully
GG : Green Gallery
P : Pinnacle
GW : Great Wall

ET : Eastern Terrace
M : Middle Rock

B : The Boulder
WT : Western Terrace
SB : Steep Band

Traditional Cloggy apprenticeships begin on East Buttress cracks, and mature on West Buttress slabs. It serves us well, but nothing can fully prepare us for that momentous stride from pre-war Sunset Crack on to post-war Llithrig wall. A second's encouragement helps initially, but on turning the arête there is only a grey wall for company. Not that there's much time for reflection while grappling with the complexities of a *5a* traverse and the logistics of a subsequent pendulum.

Llithrig ends in deceptive cracks and corners, but already the Pinnacle looms. The Taurus groove cuts up its left edge from a shattered base. Pinnacle Arête borrows its first ten metres. Not a difficult groove by Cloggy standards, but there is no protection. Stay cool, and look forward to draping arms and slings over huge flakes on the traverse.

A hard move wins the arête, renews exposure, and invites the crux. Fingers burrow into a thin crack alongside good runners, while eyes fix on a spike above. Hard luck if it happens to be loose! (It is.) Now breeze the traverse, assuming you have chosen the best line, and jitter up the wobbly groove beyond. Suddenly it's all over. Incredible but true.

# 55: PIGOTT'S CLIMB (VS+) 85m & CHIMNEY ROUTE (VS) 110m

**Summary:** The original East Buttress crack climbs, full of character but increasingly neglected in favour of predictable difficulties on Curving or Pedestal. Good, old-fashioned struggles spiced with occasional technicalities.

**First Ascent:** Pigott's – A. S. Pigott, M. Wood, L. Henshaw and J. F. Burton, May 1927; Chimney Route – C. F. Kirkus and J. M. Edwards, August 1931.

**Best Conditions:** North facing at 750m. Both routes climb deep fissures which remain damp for several days after bad weather, even in high summer. Rarely in condition outside the main summer season.

**Approach:** As for Route 54. Refer to Snowdon Area map. 1hr.

**Starting Point:** At the lower left side of the East Buttress, on ledges below the respective corner lines. Refer to Route 54 crag diagram.

**Descent:** Pigott's emerges on the Green Gallery below the Pinnacle. Escape rightwards up short walls and terraces to Eastern Terrace, and descend as for Route 53. Chimney Route joins this escape route shortly before the terrace.

Much of the appeal of Pigott's derives from its historical associations. It was the first route to breach the East Buttress, and the first major ascent on Cloggy. Imagine Pigott and Henshaw having to retreat from the '10-foot corner' for lack of a third person to complete a human pyramid; or Morley Wood on the main crack, swarming over Henshaw while he clung precariously to a threaded chockstone; or Pigott, secured by 'six feet of Beale', heaving himself exhausted on to the upper ledges during the fourth and successful attempt.

The Abrahams attempted the line of Chimney Route as early as 1905, but it took that formidable and rare partnership of Kirkus and Edwards before any real impression could be made on this imposing fissure. They struggled over grass and loose rock, and took the Rickety Innards overhang direct. Today the chimney gives a fine bridging pitch on clean rock, while the Innards are avoided by the wonderfully exposed upper groove and wall of Diglyph. Only the Continuation Chimney can recapture some of the dismal atmosphere and insecurity of the original ascent. Not to be missed.

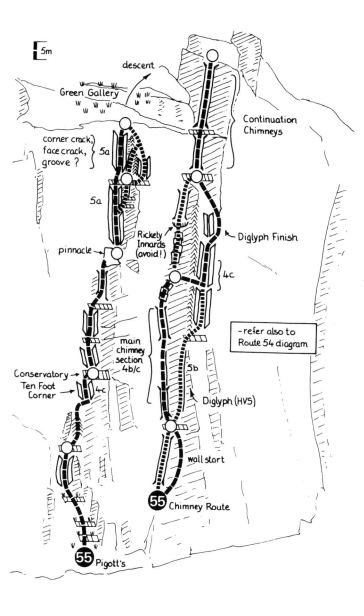

5m

descent

Green Gallery

corner crack,
face crack,
groove ? } 5a

5a

pinnacle

Rickety
Innards
(avoid!)

Conservatory
Ten Foot
Corner

4c

main
chimney
section
4b/c

Continuation
Chimneys

Diglyph Finish

4c

- refer also to
Route 54 diagram

5b

Diglyph (HVS)

wall start

**55** Chimney Route

**55** Pigott's

# 56: CURVING CRACK (VS) 65m & VEMBER (E1) 95m

**Summary:** Typical East Buttress crack climbing, on which stamina and resting ability are as important as jamming and bridging skills. Protection mostly good, except for the start of Vember (wide nut useful here).

**First Ascent:** Curving Crack – C. F. Kirkus, M. Linnell and party, June 1932; Vember – J. Brown and D. Whillans, October 1951 (A. Birtwistle climbed the Drainpipe Crack in 1937).

**Best Conditions:** North facing at 750m. Both routes are slow to dry, and the Drainpipe Crack rarely dries completely.

**Approach:** As for Route 54. Refer to Snowdon Area map. 1hr.

**Starting Point:** Curving – ascend a glacis rightwards to the foot of a 10m right-facing corner. Vember – on ledges above the lower left end of the glacis, below an obvious wide crack.

**Descent:** Down Eastern Terrace as for Route 53.

Curving Crack held out until 1932. Maurice Linnell solved the entry problem; climbing solo, he laybacked up a hidden corner crack, and pulled out on to the elusive ledge, whereupon he courteously handed over the lead to Kirkus.

Superior footwear has transformed Linnell's entry into an enjoyable jamming pitch. From the ledge a bold swing accesses the sinister chimney-groove, which soon eases to a stance shared with Vember on the left wall. The upper corner, reputedly less difficult, in fact relents only after some determined climbing.

Vember begins directly up the Drainpipe Crack. Disconcertingly wide, and invariably wet, this infamous fissure presents the leader with a dilemma. Is it best to jam or layback? A compromise semi-layback seems to be effective – provided you can maintain it for six or seven metres without protection.

The big pitch follows a series of cracks and shallow chimneys in the wall left of Curving. The crux involves working up a very shallow slot – bridging, back-and-footing (in a two-dimensional sense), and anything else that happens to work. Good protection permits experimentation – a luxury denied Joe Brown who, falling from this pitch during the first unsuccessful attempt in 1950, came to rest on the grass rake, his hemp rope almost severed.

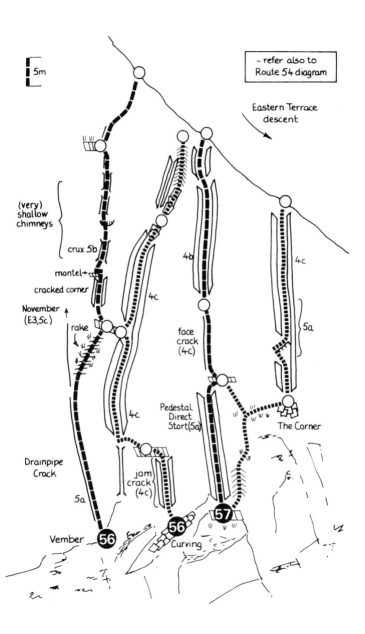

5m

- refer also to Route 54 diagram

Eastern Terrace descent

(very) shallow chimneys

crux 5b

mantel →

cracked corner

November (E3,5c) ↑

rake

4b

4c

4c

face crack (4c)

4c

Pedestal Direct Start(5a)

The Corner

Drainpipe Crack

jam crack (4c)

5a

Vember **56**

**56** Curving

**57**

5a

4c

# 57: PEDESTAL CRACK DIRECT (VS+) & THE CORNER (HVS) 60m

**Summary:** East Buttress jamming at its best. Energetic and technical. Good protection throughout. The Corner compares favourably with Cenotaph Corner. Illustrated on Route 56 diagram.

**First Ascent:** Pedestal Crack – C. F. Kirkus and G. G. Macphee, August 1931 (Direct Start – C. F. Kirkus and M. Linnell, 1932); The Corner – J. Brown, J. R. Allen and D. Belshaw, June 1952.

**Best Conditions:** North facing at 750m. Both routes follow corner cracks, and so require several fine summer days to dry out after prolonged bad weather.

**Approach:** As for Route 54. Refer to Snowdon Area map. 1hr.

**Starting Point:** At the foot of an obvious left-facing corner rising from the upper right end of a glacis. Refer to Route 56 diagram.

**Descent:** Both routes finish low down on Eastern Terrace. Descend as for Route 53.

The direct start to Pedestal Crack defeated Kirkus on his first attempt. Undeterred, he found a way on to the Pedestal front, and finished up grass to a stance at its top. Clearly dissatisfied with this solution he returned the following year with Linnell and forced a direct line, thus establishing the hardest crack pitch on Cloggy. Its *'Extremely Severe'* tag was rationalised long ago, but the pitch still requires a purposeful approach. The original crux – a ten metre face crack above the Pedestal tip – seems no easier. However, good protection eases tension and in doing so frees arms and legs to get on with the job of securing the best jams. Gritstoners will eat this crack for breakfast.

The Corner, short but pure, ascends the right-hand major feature of the East Buttress. Some people say, though not in public, that it makes a better climb than Cenotaph! Of several possible approaches, the Direct Start to Pedestal is closest in character to the main pitch (although the impatient will settle for half the original Pedestal start and a short grass traverse). Not that it matters – it's getting there that counts. And what a line! Brown led it in socks on a wet day, gouging dripping sods from the crack as he went. Today it yields to controlled jamming and bridging, supplemented by the occasional burst of effort to help overcome a lean section.

# 58: THE BOULDER (HVS) 110m

**Summary:** A lonely lead in tremendous position up the front of the Boulder. Technically reasonable but poorly protected climbing. Not recommended for those of excitable disposition. Illustrated on Route 59 diagram.

**First Ascent:** J. Brown (unseconded), October 1951.

**Best Conditions:** North facing at 800m. After rain the open, slabby walls of the Boulder dry faster than most others on the cliff. However, difficulty will increase dramatically in poor conditions because of sloping, lichenous holds.

**Approach:** As for Route 54 to the foot of the East Buttress. Scramble up to the right to arrive on Eastern Terrace below the Boulder, a featureless expanse of rock on the left side of the West Buttress. Refer to Snowdon Area map. 1hr.

**Starting Point:** Below the left edge of the slabby front face.

**Descent:** Scramble up the couloir to level ground above the buttress. Walk left and descend steep grass and scree on to Eastern Terrace. Descend as for Route 53.

The Boulder doesn't fit into the accepted order of things on Cloggy, having neither the slabs of the West nor the cracks of the East. But it is too big to ignore; glance up at its pitted face once too often and curiosity will get the better of you.

An introductory section of no particular difficulty leads in ten metres or so to a small ledge. Those who want the moral support of a nearby belay will hoist their reluctant seconds up to this stance. Otherwise, clip the pegs for protection and embark at once on the rising traverse towards Black Cleft.

The crux arrives almost at once. Holds improve after five metres, but not the protection. Place four good runners on this entire pitch and you can be well satisfied. Ron Moseley faced a massive pendulum into Black Cleft during the first ascent and quite rightly refused to follow Brown's lead. Fix a back rope unless you want to repeat Brown's epic ascent.

Black Cleft saves a sharp little overhang to share with The Boulder. It was here that Brown, having asked for another rope to be tied on so he could finish the climb, almost came to grief when his anorak hood caught on a down-pointing spike. Observant leaders with no sense of history will discover an easier breach three metres left.

# 59: LONGLAND'S CLIMB (VS) 110m

**Summary:** Pleasant climbing on steep slabs, with a scary finish on overhanging rock above the Crevasse Stance. The original and easiest climb on the West Buttress, but not one to be underestimated. Mostly adequate protection.

**First Ascent:** J. L. Longland, A. S. Pigott and party, Whit 1928.

**Best Conditions:** North facing at 800m. Allow several fine days after bad weather. Not likely to be found in condition between November and April.

**Approach:** As for Route 54 to the foot of the East Buttress. Refer to Snowdon Area map. Scramble up to the right to arrive on Eastern Terrace below the Boulder. Descend rightwards along the continuation of Eastern Terrace to the foot of Black Cleft – an evil corner between the Boulder and the West Buttress proper. Some parties may wish to rope up here. Scramble up a small gully then traverse right to a huge flake. Descend slightly and move right, around the arête, to below a slender slab. 1hr 15mins.

**Starting Point:** At the foot of the slab (or on Eastern Terrace).

**Descent:** Scramble to the top, then descend Eastern Terrace as for Route 58.

In all of Britain there is no expanse of rock more beautiful than the sheaf of overlapping slabs on Cloggy's West Buttress. After Pigott's success on the East Buttress, in 1927, it was only natural that the best rock climbers of the day should focus their attention on this next great challenge. But would they be able to force a route through the band of shattered overhangs which undercuts its entire length? Longland, prospecting with Geoffrey Winthrop Young and Frank Smythe, surveyed the problem from the terrace beneath but could find no feasible entry. Instead, he climbed a dripping wall below Eastern Terrace, and discovered a simple flanking route on to the slabs. Longland and Smythe returned two days later and, in the hours before rain stopped play, excavated what is now the first slab pitch. Working independently, Pigott's team also discovered the side entry. However, confronted by the evidence of a previous attempt they lost heart just above Smythe's high point and retreated. But their presence on the West Buttress had not gone unnoticed. Longland was tipped off and next day the two parties converged on the cliff, joined forces in the true spirit of mountaineering, and made history.

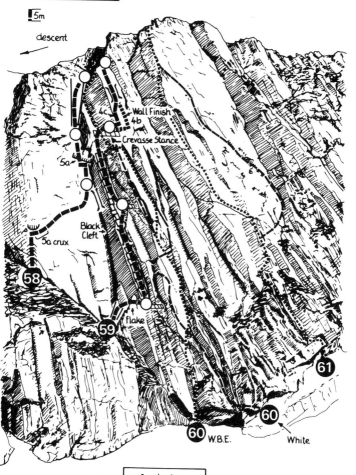

Clogwyn du'r Arddu
– West Buttress

5m

descent

4c
Wall Finish
4b
Crevasse Stance
5a
5a crux
Black Cleft
58
59
Flake
61
60
60 W.B.E.
White

-refer also to
Route 54 diagram

## 60: WHITE SLAB (E1) & WEST BUTTRESS ELIMINATE (E2) 175m

**Summary:** Magnificent expeditions based on the finest West Buttress slab. Difficult entries win elegant slab pitches and, on the Eliminate, an awesome back-and-foot groove. Protection mostly adequate, except on the two main slab pitches of White.

**First Ascent:** White – R. Moseley and J. Smith, April 1956; Eliminate – B. Ingle and P. Crew, June 1962 (Walsh's Groove – P. Walsh, 1959).

**Best Conditions:** North facing at 800m. White Slab should dry within a couple of fine summer days; the Eliminate – and Walsh's Groove in particular – will take much longer.

**Approach:** As for Route 54 to the foot of the East Buttress. Continue traversing at a lower level, passing below Middle Rock, to arrive below the undercut base of the West Buttress. Refer to Snowdon Area map. 1hr.

**Starting Point:** White: at a shattered pillar near the lower left end of Western Terrace. Eliminate: at a reddish groove almost directly below the White Slab itself. Refer to Route 59 diagram.

**Descent:** Scramble to the top and descend Eastern Terrace as for Route 58.

Linnell, *in extremis*, leapt across the base of White Slab while approaching Narrow Slab in 1933. In later years Birtwistle, Edwards, Cambell, and Harding, each reluctantly repeated Linnell's manoeuvre after being rejected by the bald Siren herself.

When Joe Brown took up the challenge in the fifties he created a new entry over the undercut base – but only after failing on the red groove now taken by the Eliminate. After reversing Linnell's Leap he climbed past Harding's high point on the big slab, solved the delicate crux, and moved left to belay in Ghecko Groove (then unclimbed). A higher traverse returned him to the arête but he saw no means of continuing the climb up the blank slab.

Brown and Moseley returned a few days later and overcame the impasse by lassoing a small spike they had seen in the far corner of the slab (a line later followed by the Eliminate).

Two years later Moseley completed the route by moving rightwards into a fierce V-groove. Three years later this entire groove was climbed by Patsy Walsh in mistake for Sheaf; 'Walsh's Groove' subsequently became the highlight of the Eliminate.

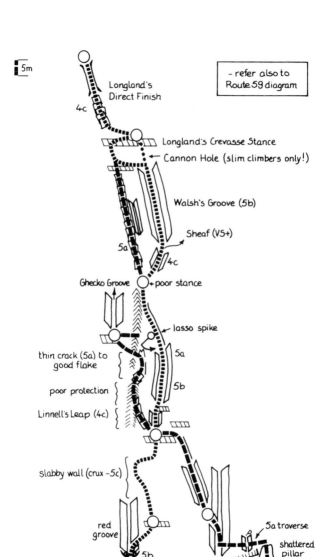

- refer also to
Route 59 diagram

Longland's
Direct Finish

4c

Longland's Crevasse Stance

Cannon Hole (slim climbers only!)

Walsh's Groove (5b)

Sheaf (VS+)

5a

4c

Ghecko Groove

poor stance

lasso spike

thin crack (5a) to
good flake

5a

poor protection

5b

Linnell's Leap (4c)

slabby wall (crux –5c)

red
groove

5b

5a traverse

shattered
pillar

60 W.B.E.

60 White

5m

# 61: GREAT/BOW COMBINATION (VS+) 170m

**Summary:** A long, taxing climb suitable only for skilful partnerships; the biggest and best of Cloggy's easier routes. This combination of entry and upper slab pitches maintains a high level of interest. Adequate protection, except at the crucial Bow Traverse. Double ropes strongly recommended.

**First Ascent:** Great Slab – C. F. Kirkus and G. G. Macphee, June 1930; Bow-Shaped Slab – J. M. Edwards and J. Cooper, September 1941.

**Best Conditions:** North facing at 800m. Most of the climb follows open slabs which, in summer, will dry within a few days of bad weather. Rarely in condition between November and April.

**Approach:** As for Route 60 to the foot of Western Terrace. Refer to Snowdon Area map. 1hr.

**Starting Point:** About 50m along Western Terrace, where a pinnacle bridges the gap between terrace and undercut slab. Refer to Route 59 diagram.

**Descent:** Scramble to the top, and descend Eastern Terrace as for Route 58.

The Great entry was the first to breach the main barrier of West Buttress overhangs. Longland and Pigott had been here in 1928, prior to discovering the side entry to their climb. But whereas they had attempted a direct line, Kirkus and Macphee side-stepped down to the left and entered a more hopeful slabby groove. In residence at that time was the downwardly mobile Green Caterpillar (since evicted to reveal a comforting flake crack). On reaching the main slab, Kirkus tried without success to climb its left edge, and eventually settled for a rightward traverse into the Forty-Foot Corner – key to the easier upper slabs.

Ten years later a wandering and now neglected entry brought Menlove Edwards to a junction with Great Slab. Like Kirkus, he also tried and failed to climb the bow-shaped indentation. Undeterred, he continued above Great's shallow pillar and traversed the Bow along a diagonal line of weakness. Climbers today take a slightly easier high line when beginning the traverse (feet on the fault line, back rope or high runner for the second), but even they must make some breath-holding shuffles in search of poor side holds. Incidentally, Bow-Shaped Slab was not repeated for seven years.

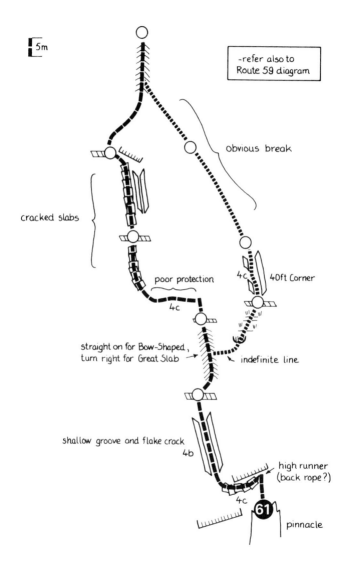

5m

-refer also to
Route 59 diagram

obvious break

cracked slabs

40ft Corner

4c

poor protection

4c

straight on for Bow-Shaped,
turn right for Great Slab

indefinite line

shallow groove and flake crack

4b

high runner
(back rope?)

4c

61

pinnacle

# 62: OXINE (VS+) 60m

**Summary:** The best combination of pitches up the main face of a pleasantly situated valley crag. Bold climbing up vertical rock on good holds. Adequate protection for the difficult sections.

**First Ascent:** Oxo – J. R. Lees, G. D. Roberts and W. A. Trench, April 1953; Bovine – C. E. Davies, B. D. Wright and D. McKelvey, May 1957.

**Best Conditions:** A low-lying crag, the Wenallt faces south-east and so dries quickly after rain. Climbable at any time of year. A cool option for warm summer evenings (but beware the evil midge!).

**Approach:** Follow the A498 Beddgelert to Capel Curig road to a junction at GR.651 523, just north of Llyn Gwynant. Turn down here (steep lane) and after about 100m turn left along a track. Park at its terminus near the head of the lake. Cross the river by a footbridge a few hundred metres upstream and go left along the riverside path. Ascend steeply up a boulder field to the crag. Refer to Snowdon Area map. GR.647 527. 20mins.

**Starting Point:** There is a huge boulder at the foot of the crag. Start up to the left, where an obvious rightward traverse line leads out across the face (use the prominent corners of Bovine to help confirm correct location).

**Descent:** Continue to the top of the buttress and descend steep slopes to the left of the crag.

The bleached bastion of Clogwyn y Wenallt, pine-clad at its base, rises incongruously from the lakeland beauty of Nant Gwynant like a hairy wart. It is not a pretty crag.

Bovine gets hopelessly mixed up with holdless corners on its first pitch. Oxo, meanwhile, discovers a lucky sequence of flakes and gangways. The situation reverses itself on the upper wall: Oxo scuttles off to the left while Bovine addresses the main challenge. Oxine, therefore, becomes the definitive hybrid.

But what about this upper wall? It hardly looks climbable at *Extreme*, let alone *VS*. Tentative probing at a slender groove merely confirms these fears. Nothing for it then but to quit the groove, launch out on the face to its right, and hope for the best. And the best is what you get: an escalator of super-jugs leading up to the summit. All you need is the agility to jump aboard, and the stamina to hold on.

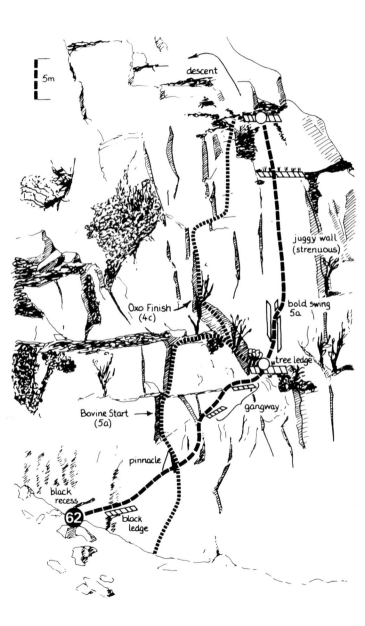

5m

descent

juggy wall
(strenuous)

Oxo Finish
(4c)

bold swing
5a

tree ledge

gangway

Bovine Start
(5a)

pinnacle

black
recess

**62**

black
ledge

# Outlying Areas

Outlying crags of North Wales are unjustifiably neglected. While none command the reputation or history of crags in central Snowdonia, the quality of climbing is in no way inferior.

The Moelwyn crags not only enjoy milder weather than those of Ogwen, but are spared their polished holds and weekend queues. In many ways, these delightful climbs on rough rock make far better introductions to rock climbing.

Craig yr Ogof in Cwm Silyn is a major crag in its own right, with a full complement of classics from *D* to *E2* on reliable rock. A remote setting enhances its appeal. The fierce low-lying outcrop of Castell Cidwm extends opportunities in this region.

There is no point pretending that the routes selected from Cader Idris and Aran accurately represent the usual type of climbing in Central Wales. Many crags look promising, only to disappoint on close approach. Nevertheless, several excellent climbs await the connoisseur, a few of which are included here. Among them are a couple of winter climbs which rank alongside the very best in Wales.

**Approaches:** Crags in this section lie to the south or east of major climbing areas, from where they may be approached on a daily basis.

**Accommodation and Services:** Refer to listings under main area headings. The following information may be useful to those intending to base themselves locally.

Alltrem & Moelwyn crags: *Camping*, unofficially, in Cwm Orthin; *Youth Hostels* in Ffestiniog and near Dolwyddelan (Lledr Valley); other services in Dolwyddelan and Blaenau Ffestiniog.

Cidwm & Craig yr Ogof: *Camping* at an official forestry site, 1.5km north-west of Beddgelert near A4085 (GR.578 491); *Youth Hostel* near Rhyd Ddu (Snowdon Ranger); other accommodation and services at Beddgelert, Rhyd Ddu and Pen y Groes.

Cader Idris: *Camping* near A487 (GR.738 120); *Youth Hostel* (Kings); other accommodation and services in Dolgellau.

Aran group: *Camping* 1km south of Dinas Mawddwy near A470 (GR.860 139); *Youth Hostel* at Bala; other accommodation and services in Dinas Mawddwy, Llanuwchllyn and Bala.

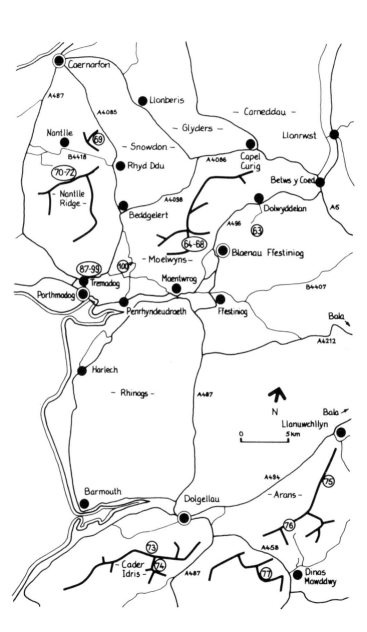

*Ramp section on Ordinary Route (Route 70), Cwm Silyn.*

*On the exposed arete of Acheron (Route 76), Craig Cywarch.*

# 63: LAVAREDO (VS+) & LIGHTNING VISIT (VS) 45m

**Summary :** Exhilarating climbing on a pleasantly situated outcrop. A bold approach gets results. Good runners, except on the top pitch of Lavaredo.

**First Ascent:** Lavaredo – R. James, K. Forder and I. F. Campbell, March 1961; Lightning Visit – R. James and C. T. Jones, June 1959.

**Best Conditions:** Faces west at low altitude and so dries quickly after rain. Climbing possible at any time of year, but best on a spring or autumn evening.

**Approach:** In Dolwyddelan turn south at crossroads, cross the river, and fork right over a railway bridge. Turn right immediately and follow a narrow lane for 1.5km, passing two gates, to a small parking bay about 100m beyond the second. Follow a path left, across the stream, to a forestry track. Ascend through trees to a second forestry track below the crag. Refer to Outlying Areas map for general location. GR.739 507. 10mins. A permit may be required from the Forestry Commission office, Llanrwst.

**Starting Point:** A deep, right-facing corner (Penamnen Groove) makes a useful landmark. Lavaredo starts about 10m right, below a shallow square-cut slot (the left side of which is in fact a semi-detached rib), while Lightning Visit starts in a shallow groove 4–5m left.

**Descent:** Descend steeply on the right side of the crag, initially down a gully then on scree (this is the second gully encountered, the first being steep and insecure).

The outlook from Carreg Alltrem is rural rather than mountainous. Smoke curls from chimneys in the nearby village; a chain-saw rasps intermittently in the forest below. Any sense of urgency is reserved for moments of commitment on the routes themselves.

Climbing these pale walls evokes the limestone experience. Fingers curl over a sharp-edged flake, feet edge sideways on square-cut holds; is that another good jug above? Only one way to find out: settle the tape runner, bunch up on high footholds, and go for it. Outrageously exposed Lavaredo rewards every brave reach, but one, with another good hold.

But Alltrem is about corners too. Penamnen Groove (*HVS*), immediately recognisable by its twisting off-width, ought to be the best route on the crag. In the event, it stutters to a grunting halt. Lightning Visit, apart from a puzzling entry to an upper groove, capitulates with more grace and a lot less effort.

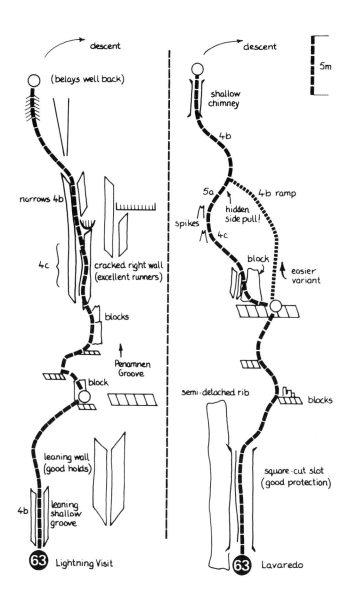

descent

(belays well back)

narrows 4b

4c

cracked right wall
(excellent runners)

blocks

Penamnen
Groove

block

leaning wall
(good holds)

4b    leaning
shallow
groove

**63** Lightning Visit

descent

5m

shallow
chimney

4b

5a          4b ramp

hidden
side pull!

spikes

4c

block

easier
variant

semi-detached rib

blocks

square-cut slot
(good protection)

**63** Lavaredo

# 64: ASAHEL/EAGLE FINISH (VS) 50m

**Summary:** Pleasant climbing on positive, quartz holds, to an airy finish above overhangs. The crux is well protected. A charming crag despite sordid surroundings. Rarely crowded.

**First Ascent:** Asahel – R. James and R. L. Roberts, July 1955; Eagle Finish – J. R. Lees and K. C. Gordon, April 1961.

**Best Conditions:** Faces south at an altitude of 400m. Dries quickly after rain. Very pleasant in spring and autumn, but also on fine winter days.

**Approach:** From the crossroads in Tan y Grisiau, follow the steep lane (which passes beneath the narrow-gauge railway) to a parking space at the end of its surfaced section. Continue on foot up the Cwm Orthin track to quarry ruins. Turn sharp right and ascend inclines among slate spoil to the crag. Refer to Outlying Areas map for general location, and Route 67 map for details of approach. GR.683 458. 25mins.

**Starting Point:** The right-hand section of the crag is made up of slabs and corners topped by steep walls. Start below the right side of the large quartz slab.

**Descent:** Down a grassy couloir on the left side of the crag.

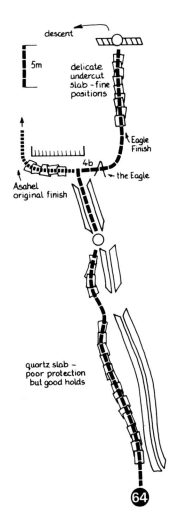

descent

5m

delicate
undercut
slab - fine
positions

Eagle
Finish

4b

the Eagle

Asahel
original finish

quartz slab –
poor protection
but good holds

**64**

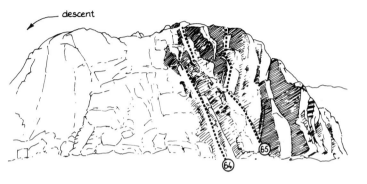

Craig y Clipiau

descent

Huge piles of slate spoil threaten to engulf Craig y Clipiau in blue-grey splinters. But the crag rises proudly above its dismal surroundings, quartz slabs glistening in the sun. A rockery and small lawn, tended by wayward sheep, obstinately intervenes between crag front and quarry highway.

The average standard of good climbing on Clipiau is higher than is typical of other Moelwyn crags. Pocketed rock can still be found, but only at a steeper angle. The white slab of Asahel is an obvious feature of the crag. Several routes take advantage of its positive holds: Africa Rib (*VD*) wanders pleasantly up its left edge; Brys (*HVS*) climbs directly up its centre to exit through a groove in capping overhangs; while Asahel finds security and some protection near its right-hand corner.

Overhangs force Asahel out left to an unremarkable finish near Africa Rib. However, an exciting possibility reveals itself where the overhang arches down to form the right retaining wall of the slab. A wide bridge and bold pull gets you within grabbing distance of a stone eagle's neck. Provided it doesn't flutter away unexpectedly, you now have the means (and protection) to turn the overhang and enjoy the pleasant hanging slab beyond.

# 65: MEAN FEET (VS+) 40m

**Summary:** An unusual outcrop climb of outstanding quality. Excellent protection on the crucial V-groove. Perfect rock.

**First Ascent:** R. James and P. Vaughan, July 1957.

**Best Conditions:** As for Route 64, although the V-groove will take longer to dry.

**Approach:** As for Route 64.

**Starting Point:** Below a vegetated corner on the right side of a convex slab (which is topped by an overhanging wall). Refer to Route 64 crag drawing.

**Descent:** Down a grassy couloir on the left side of the crag.

To the right of Asahel slab, the upper half of the crag tilts up to wall angle and beyond, while its supporting plinth – though slabby – exhibits a precise smoothness. Mean Feet cunningly exploits a superb flake crack in the angle between these two features.

It takes courage to set off on such a prolonged hand traverse. It could be difficult, but it isn't. Instead it delivers you quickly to a tiny stance below the crucial V-groove. Beneath your feet the rock curls away into overhangs, emphasising the isolated position. Glance up to the right if you dare and imagine yourself bridged across the hanging groove of Crimson Cruiser (*E5*).

A couple of well-placed pocket holds invite entry to the V-groove. Perfect runners drop into place from a comfortable bridging rest. It could be easy, but it isn't: someone forgot to put an intermediate handhold between the last good bit of the crack, and first good grip on the finishing flake. A runner at chin level offers some moral support, but the lunge from one to the other will be the single hardest move of the route. Keep the adrenalin pumping if you can, because there's a puzzling little wall to finish.

Assuming a successful encounter with Mean Feet, Craig y Clipiau will entertain until sunset with a couple of other little gems. These are illustrated opposite. Inverted Staircase (*VS*) is just that, but not a place to linger despite huge holds. A pocketed wall above elicits fond memories of Wrysgan and Oen. Double Criss (*VS+*) begins with a fine wall and rib pitch on incuts. However, the rib narrowly fails to escape encroaching side walls. The climb will be won or lost on those few metres of brutally overhanging fist crack. The odds are not good.

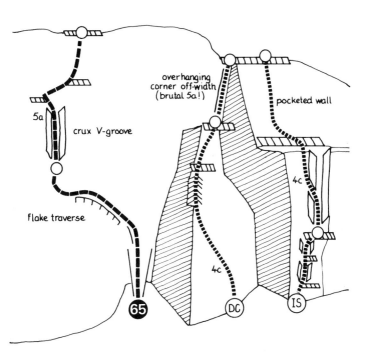

5m

Craig y Clipiau
- right hand section

overhanging
corner off-width
(brutal 5a!)

pocketed wall

5a

crux V-groove

4c

flake traverse

4c

65

DC

IS

- refer also to
Route 64 diagram

# 66: Y GELYNEN/HONEYSUCKLE CORNER (S) 90m

**Summary:** Delicate and poorly protected rib climbing, followed by a strenuous but safe corner. The crag is pleasantly situated in a relatively unfrequented part of North Wales.

**First Ascent:** Y Gelynen – R. Davies and G. Williams, July 1953; Honeysuckle Corner – J. R. Lees and G. Moffat – April 1961.

**Best Conditions:** The crag faces south-east at an altitude of 400m. Slabby areas dry quickly after rain, although Honeysuckle Corner will remain damp for a day or so longer. Can also be pleasant on fine winter days.

**Approach:** As for Route 64 to ruined quarry buildings. Cross the stream on the left and contour left to the foot of the crag. Alternatively, approach as for Route 67 along the Stwlan Dam road, and ascend direct. Refer to Outlying Areas map for general location, and Route 67 map for details of approach. GR.679 454. 20mins.

**Starting Point:** Below a grass ledge under the V-groove of Dorcon (refer to crag drawing).

**Descent:** Cross into a pit beyond the crag top and descend the tunnel incline. Finally bear left (looking out) to regain the foot of the cliff.

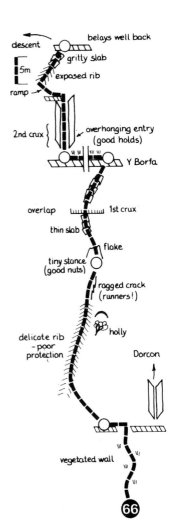

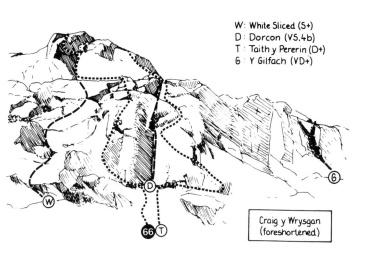

W : White Sliced (S+)
D : Dorcon (VS,4b)
T : Taith y Pererin (D+)
6 : Y Gilfach (VD+)

Craig y Wrysgan
(foreshortened)

Grass and heather cement the stonework joints of Craig Yr Wrysgan, which accounts for its rather shabby appearance. Barren Ogwen crags must have looked something like this before nailed boots stripped them clean and buffed their holds to a polish. Today even the most popular Moelwyn classic retains much of its original character.

Pumice-textured rock is a great comfort on Y Gelynen. A few runners can be fiddled into the larger pock-holes of the rib, but it will be the profusion of sharp-edged pockets which provides the greater encouragement. The crux arrives at a small overlap on the slab pitch. Although technically no harder than some previous moves, an exposed situation and off-balance execution add an extra dash of seriousness.

Impetus for the climb evaporates on the luxurious terrace of Y Borfa (a good place for lunch, except that lunch is in a rucksack at the bottom of the crag). A separate and dissimilar finish up Honeysuckle Corner completes the dislocation. The corner overhangs alarmingly at first, but the holds are huge and the angle soon relents. An airy finish restores some of the original perspectives of the climb, only to have them unhinged by a novel subterranean descent.

# 67: KIRKUS'S CLIMB DIRECT (VD+) 85m

**Summary:** A direct line based on the first recorded climb in the district. Perhaps the most enjoyable climb in the Moelwyns. Includes a wide variety of both strenuous and delicate passages, all of which are on excellent bubbly rock. Adequate protection. There are numerous easier but inferior variations.

**First Ascent:** C. F. Kirkus and C. G. Kirkus, 1928.

**Best Conditions:** As for Route 68. The chimney start to pitch three may be slow to dry.

**Approach:** As for Route 64 to the parking bay. Refer to Outlying Areas map for general location, and the map opposite for details of approach. Fork left immediately from the Cwm Orthin track, and cross the footbridge to join the surfaced (but private) Stwlan Dam road beyond the stream. Follow the road uphill for almost 1km to boulders below the crag. GR.674 449. 30mins.

**Starting Point:** A blunt rib defines the left side of the slabby front face. Start at its foot, beneath an overhanging wall.

**Descent:** Traverse leftwards along ledges and enter an easy scree gully which bounds the crag on its left.

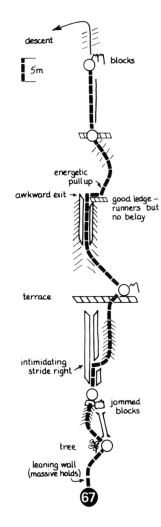

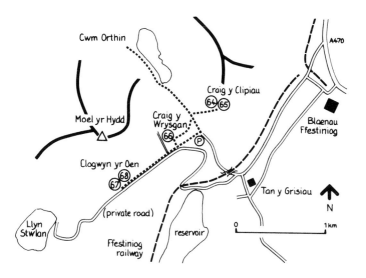

When viewed from the road, Clogwyn yr Oen appears to lack the distinctive features that might lend character and individuality to its climbs. An area of slabs central to the cliff upholds this view. However, a closer study of rock to right and left suggests a more complex structure. This will be fully revealed only as the climbs progress.

Five metres of overhanging wall hardly seems a proper way to begin a pleasant *V.Diff*. Massive holds compensate, but even so this is no time for indecisive climbing. Although not a preferred Moelwyn technique, dynamism proves equally effective when swinging out to regain the main rib line from three metres up the variant chimney. Be assured, the climb will henceforth restrict itself to genuine Moelwyn balance climbing.

Undoubtedly the highlight of the Direct is a grooved rib above the half-way terrace. Slender and exposed, the groove delivers you on to a perfectly situated ledge on the front of the rib – highly recommended to those given to smoking pipes and philosophising. Sadly, the belays are inadequate, and so after a brief pause for poetic reflection there is no alternative but to set off in search of a better appointed stance.

# 68: SLICK (VD) & SLACK (S) 100m

**Summary:** Pleasant, if unremarkable, climbing lifted from obscurity by well-positioned crux pitches: a delicate slab on Slick, and an intimidating arête on Slack. Adequate protection.

**First Ascent:** Slick – A. J. J. Moulam, J. A. F. Watson and R. G. Hargreaves, April 1953; Slack – I. F. Cartledge and J. R. Lees, November 1960.

**Best Conditions:** The crag faces south-east at an altitude of 400m. A very pleasant venue on sunny days, in summer or winter. Dries quickly, although drainage can affect corners and overlaps after bad weather. When wet, a coating of lichen on the rock drastically reduces the normally excellent friction.

**Approach:** As for Route 67.

**Starting Point:** A blunt rib (climbed by Route 67) defines the left side of the slabby front face. From its foot, ascend grass terraces rightwards, for about 50m, to a ledge below a slightly recessed area of slabs. Slick starts from a sandy grotto at the foot of a 20m cracked rib. Slack starts about 15m further right, below slabs leading to a ledge and huge flake at 30m.

**Descent:** Traverse leftwards, along ledges, to enter an easy scree gully which bounds the crag on its left.

Moelwyn crags are not much to look at; the impressive architecture of Idwal or Cwm Silyn is absent. In its place you have the bizarre panorama of slate hillside, toy town railway, artificial lake, reclaimed spoil heap, and nuclear power-station. From time to time a coach load of tourists returning from the Stwlan Dam will pass within hailing distance of the crag, their gesticulations adding a final brush stroke of surrealism to the scene.

In contrast, the climbing on Slick and Slack is earthy and predictable, at least up to a point. Initially, each climb unrolls as a familiar pattern of slabby walls and grass ledges. Nothing extraordinary, nothing too difficult. The upset comes later. Plodding, unremarkable Slack suddenly darts off left, beneath an overhang, and begins shoving you up a vertical arête. Down to the left, you might see an equally bemused leader confronted by a bald patch on Slick. Your respective challenges could hardly be more dissimilar, while your hopes and fears will be identical. One thing is certain: you'll both have plenty to talk about when you converge on the delightful top slab.

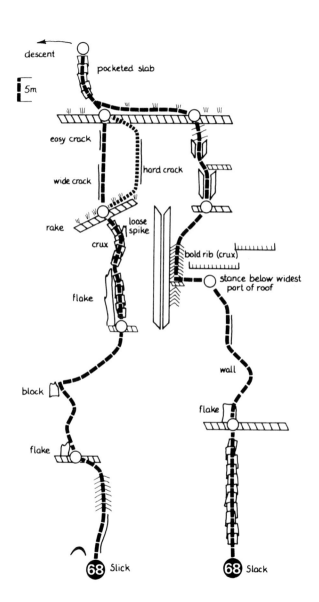

# 69: DWM (HVS/A1) 55m

**Summary:** Spectacular climbing through overhangs on a secluded outcrop. Hard for the grade. Sound rock but poor friction. Adequate protection. All aid is *in situ* (albeit rusty), but take a few extra slings.

**First Ascent:** J. Brown and H. Smith, March 1960.

**Best Conditions:** South-east facing at low altitude. Dries quickly after rain, although overlaps may weep for several days after bad weather. Climbing possible throughout the year, including sunny winter mornings.

**Approach:** A direct approach is not permitted. Instead park at Rhyd Ddu on the Beddgelert to Caernarfon road (A4085), and walk 1km north to the farm at GR.567 539. Follow a forestry track for 2km to gates. Cross the stream and wall, and ascend the pasture on the far side to the foot of the crag. Refer to Outlying Areas map for general location. GR.551 553. 40mins.

**Starting Point:** On the rake which slants rightwards beneath roofs on the right-hand side of the main wall. Refer to diagram for precise location.

**Descent:** Down the approach rake (short but difficult), or via grass slopes on the left of the crag.

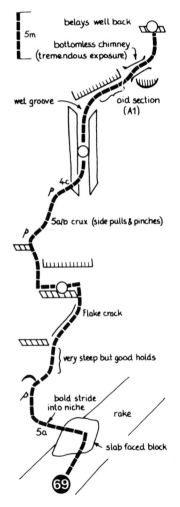

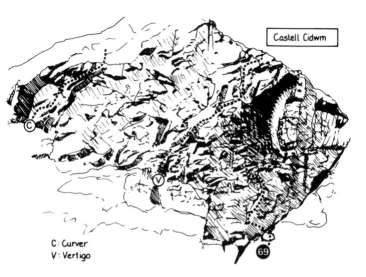

C: Curver
V: Vertigo

69

Cidwm had been explored as early as 1905, but its imposing South-East Face did not come under serious scrutiny until 1960. Joe Brown arrived on the scene, curiosity aroused by rumours of a secret crag, and in one summer picked off the three classics – Curver, Vertigo and Dwm.

Cidwm's compact and slaty rock is exceptionally difficult to predict. Add to this its tremendous exposure, quite out of proportion to its size, and you will understand why Curver (*VS+*, *4c*) and Vertigo (*VS+*, *5a*) have become popular. Nevertheless, Dwm is the major route of the three, and not be missed.

An arm-wrenching traverse into an off-balance niche sets the scene. Massive hidden jugs secure an exit and lead to the first stance. The angle of the middle pitch (merely vertical) is deceptive; its rising traverse across treacherous shelves provides the crux. Free moves in the corner begin the final pitch, but these soon degenerate into ape-like swings on aid beneath the roof. An assortment of rusting pegs and micro-wires provide support; it hardly matters how many – unless you intend climbing the pitch free at *6a*. An incredible free finish in a bottomless chimney is justification for all the trials below.

# 70: ORDINARY ROUTE (D) & OUTSIDE EDGE (VD+) 125m

**Summary:** Mountaineering routes of unusual character up the imposing prow of Craig yr Ogof. Good rock, adequate protection, exposed positions. Idyllic setting.

**First Ascent:** Ordinary – D. R. Pye, W. R. Reade, C. A. Elliot and N. E. Odell, April 1926; Outside Edge – J. M. Edwards and C. H. S. R. Palmer, July 1931.

**Best Conditions:** Although the cwm head wall generally faces north-west (at an altitude of 600m), the Great Slab cuts in at right-angles, faces south-west, and in summer catches the sun for much of the day. The Slab dries quickly after rain whereas the rock above Sunset Ledge may remain greasy for a day or so, particularly in spring or autumn.

**Approach:** As for Route 71.

**Starting Point:** Ordinary – about 10m left of the right-hand corner of Great Slab, below a low-relief triangular pedestal; Outside Edge – about 5m right of the left-hand edge of Great Slab, below an obvious hanging block.

**Descent:** (1) The Ordinary makes a fine start to a traverse of the Nantlle Ridge, otherwise (assuming sacks are carried) circle the cwm head wall rightwards and descend a gentle grass shoulder to the approach track.
(2) Return to the foot of the climbs by descending as for Route ·71.

The Great Slab looks tremendous from the approach but in reality is a little disappointing, being too steep and too smooth for proper slab climbing. Instead, the Ordinary Route struggles over a polished wall and then adheres rigidly to a series of diagonal breaks. Tedious climbing but tremendous position. Climbers on Outside Edge take a more exposed direct line, rewarded for their pluck by excellent holds on the transitional wall between reclining slab and overhanging nose.

Pitches above Sunset Ledge are more difficult and interesting. The Ordinary briefly struggles up a corner crack, and then finds a delicate slab and exposed rib; while Outside Edge ventures left towards the dark side of the prow, and ascends a series of ribs and grooves to a baffling undercut crack (clue: enter it from the right!). Those impatient for the top now scurry off to the left, while pedants and mountaineers follow the ridge direct over occasional steps and pinnacles to the barren summit plateau.

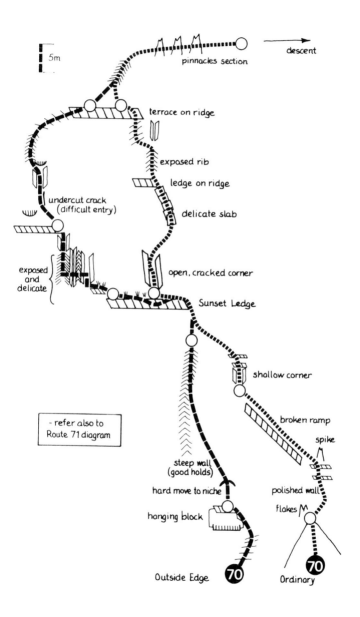

5m

descent

pinnacles section

terrace on ridge

exposed rib

ledge on ridge

delicate slab

undercut crack
(difficult entry)

open, cracked corner

exposed
and
delicate

Sunset Ledge

shallow corner

- refer also to
Route 71 diagram

broken ramp

spike

steep wall
(good holds)

hard move to niche

polished wall

hanging block

flakes

Outside Edge

70

70

Ordinary

# 71: KIRKUS'S DIRECT (VS+) 95m

**Summary:** A difficult entry and indefinite middle section lead to a delightful finish on pocketed slabs high on the face. Sketchy protection on the Direct Start (good on the left-hand alternative).

**First Ascent:** C. F. Kirkus and G. G. Macphee, May 1931; Direct Start – V. Ridgeway and party, 1951.

**Best Conditions:** As for Route 70, although water streaks may affect the Direct Start for a few days after bad weather.

**Approach:** From Nantlle on the Rhyd Ddu to Pen y Groes road (B4418). Continue west, and turn left after 2km on the Llanllyfni road. Turn left again after 1.5km and follow this single-track road for 2km to the end of the surfaced section at GR.496 511 (parking just beyond the gate). Continue on foot until the track loses itself above the Llynnau Cwm Silyn. Contour above the lakes, and ascend laboriously up scree to the foot of the Great Slab. Refer to Outlying Areas map for general location. GR.517 502. 45mins.

**Starting Point:** Direct Start – 5m left of the right hand corner of Great Slab; Left-Hand Start – 5m further left, as for the Ordinary Route (Route 70).

**Descent:** Circle right from the crag summit, and enter the Great Stone Shoot gully (identified at the top by a stone wall and fencing). When necessary avoid awkward steps in the gully by descending the rib on its left (looking out), but avoid straying into a couloir even further left.

Kirkus began with direct intentions but allowed himself to be diverted by a weeping overlap, returning to the true line along a difficult curving crack. Over the years, so many impatient climbers have scrambled up the Ordinary to begin the crack that this has now become the accepted line, thereby unintentionally conferring independent status on the beautiful slanting groove of the Direct Start. No move on the Direct is especially difficult, but the technical intricacies are sustained for several metres. Relative lack of protection enhances the experience (provided you don't fall off!).

Scope for getting lost on the upper section is limitless. A common mistake is to trend too far right, having been repulsed by the sight of apparently smooth slabs and overlaps. In fact, these are riddled with superb pocket holds – the highlight of the climb.

Craig yr Ogof

5m

# 72: CRUCIBLE (HVS) 90m & JABBERWOCKY (E2) 65m

**Summary:** Magnificent climbing on compact rock among grooves and overhangs of the Ogof Nose. Protection merely adequate. Crucible demands a steady second, Jabberwocky a brainless leader.

**First Ascent:** Crucible – B. Ingle and R. G. Wilson, June 1963; Jabberwocky – R. Evans, J. Yates and M. Yates, May 1970.

**Best Conditions:** Faces west at 600m. Dries faster than the left side of the Nose, but cracks and overlaps will weep for a day or so after bad weather.

**Approach:** As for Route 71.

**Starting Point:** Below the right-hand groove of the wall, about 5m left of Great Slab. An independent first pitch to Crucible starts beneath the large central groove of West Wall, about 15m from the left edge of Great Slab.

**Descent:** Both routes finish on Sunset Ledge. Either finish up Route 70 and descend as for Route 71, or traverse the ledge rightwards and descend the Great Slab section of Ordinary Route.

Crucible can do nothing about the great central groove of the wall and instead creeps left beneath an overhang. An aid point (wicked but traditional) gets you over the worst of it, but must be quitted almost at once for a series of brave pulls up to the left. A bit of extra rope drag comes in handy now for some illicit tension (naughty but nice) on the leftward traverse.

Nothing on Crucible is quite what it seems. The next pitch ignores most of the obvious corner which rises above, climbing instead up its left side before traversing across to finish up a poorly protected slab on the right. A capping roof brings runners but little else of comfort; the escape, out right, is precisely that.

Jabberwocky tolerates few diversions in its quest for the silvery grooved arête. A pleasant first pitch transports you quickly to a remarkable stance below its crucial groove. After a sideways entry the situation rapidly deteriorates. A series of semi-laybacks lead up past a loose hold to a gasping, grasping exit on to a hanging ramp. An exposed traverse returns you to the groove line which, having already shot its bolt, offers no more than token resistance. Climbers nursing half-way anxieties on Ordinary Route will be astonished to see you unrope on Sunset Ledge and cart-wheel past them into ecstatic oblivion.

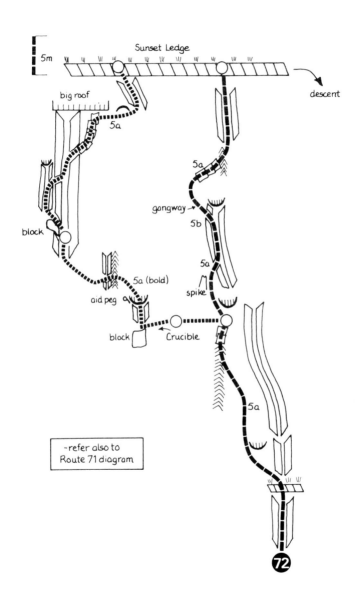

# 73: TABLE DIRECT/CYFRWY ARÊTE (D) 175m & RIB AND SLAB (S+) 140m

**Summary:** Serious mountaineering routes high on the flanks of Cader Idris. Technically uninspiring but strong on atmosphere. Some poor rock.

**First Ascent:** Cyfrwy Arête – O. G. Jones, May 1888 (Table Direct – R. E. Davies and H. E. Chatburn, June 1951); Rib and Slab – D. Burgess and J. N. Allen, June 1960.

**Best Conditions:** The main crag faces north at an altitude of 700m. It is slow to dry. The Arête is less affected by drainage and, in any case, is climbable under most conditions. Queues unlikely!

**Approach:** From Dolgellau along a minor road to the Gwernan Lake Hotel. Refer to Outlying Areas map for general location. Follow the well-marked Fox's Path to Llyn y Gadair in the cwm below Cader Idris itself. Cyfrwy Arête defines the right side of the cwm. Leave the path, cross the cwm, and ascend directly over scree towards the right side of the Arête. Refer to Route 74 map for details of approach. GR.705 135. 1hr 15mins.

**Starting Point:** Table Direct: at a ledge above the gully which rises between Table Buttress and a large pinnacle (tottering pinnacles further right). A small pinnacle lies against the wall. Rib and Slab: at the entrance to the gully which descends from the gap between the Table and the upper part of Cyfrwy Arête.

**Descent:** Continue to the summit, or descend the scree couloir left of the Arête. Refer to main text and Route 74 map for details.

The normal approach to Cyfrwy Arête sneaks in from part way up a couloir to its left (the descent couloir), arriving just below the Table. However, the inclusion of Table Direct, with its fine corner and superior rock quality, doubles the amount of interesting climbing without a significant increase in standard. Climbing the Arête itself lacks intrinsic interest but builds atmosphere wonderfully, especially at the Table and gap.

Rib and Slab has been compared to Main Wall on Cyrn Las, but frankly the rock is worrying and the climbing unattractive. Nevertheless, it has great presence and will appeal to climbers of pioneering bent.

Mountaineers will now wish to continue to the summit of Pen y Gadair by circling the rim of the cwm and joining the main tourist path. Philistines in rock boots will have to descend a scree couloir to the left of the Arête.

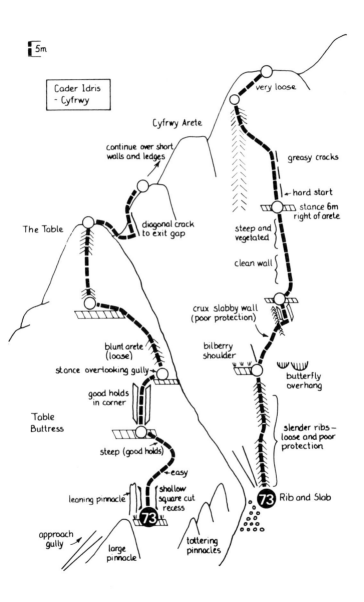

5m

Cader Idris
– Cyfrwy

Cyfrwy Arete

continue over short
walls and ledges

very loose

greasy cracks

← hard start

stance 6m
right of arete

The Table

diagonal crack
to exit gap

steep and
vegetated

clean wall

crux slabby wall
(poor protection)

blunt arete
(loose)

stance overlooking gully

bilberry
shoulder

butterfly
overhang

good holds
in corner

Table
Buttress

slender ribs –
loose and poor
protection

steep (good holds)

← easy

leaning pinnacle

shallow
square cut
recess

73 Rib and Slab

approach
gully

large
pinnacle

tottering
pinnacles

# 74: GREAT GULLY (III/IV) 250m

**Summary:** Traditional Welsh winter climbing in a remote setting. Not often in condition. Belays mostly adequate, but protection often poor.

**First Ascent:** Winter – not known; summer – O. G. Jones, E. L. W. and W. P. Haskett Smith, May 1895.

**Best Conditions:** The crag faces east at an altitude of 750m, although the gully itself faces north-east. Ice accumulation is limited, so it is worth waiting for good snow conditions.

**Approach:** From Minffordd on the A470 Dolgellau to Machynlleth road. Park opposite the Idris Gates, 300m along the B4405 towards Abergynolwyn or in the large car park near the road junction. Refer to Outlying Areas map for road approach, and map opposite for crag location at GR.712 123. 1hr 30mins.

**Starting Point:** The gully begins directly below the summit of Mynydd Pencoed, but slants leftwards to exit on the south-east ridge. It is the most prominent gully on the face, and defines the right side of Pencoed Pillar. Start below the first steep pitch.

**Descent:** Descend the ridge leftwards, circling the south side of Cwm Cau to a junction with the approach path.

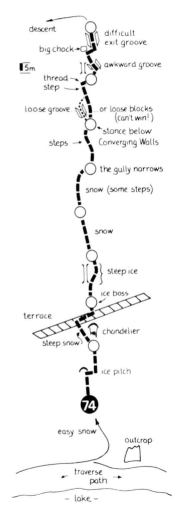

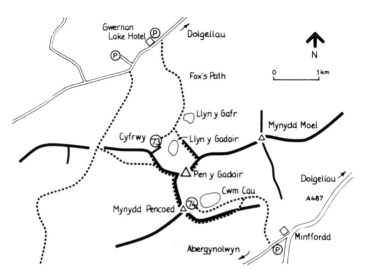

Inferior flanking variants become tempting alternatives when lean conditions impose extra difficulties on the direct line up the gully bed. They are to be resisted. Average snowfall will bank out the first chockstone pitch, but it would take a rare winter to obscure a scrattling exit from the second. Not even the summer route can do anything about the big cave below the terrace; in a typical winter its tinkling chandeliers offer no hope whatsoever. Nevertheless, it is difficult to suppress a feeling of guilt while step-kicking up easy snow on the left. No excuses for avoiding the next rise; in good conditions this produces the best ice climbing on the route.

A snowy interlude now permits a rare moment of reflection on marvellous surroundings, fully revealed for the first time – hidden cwm, frozen lake, ice-bound crag. Before long, the gully plunges into a dark cavern beneath Converging Walls. Unless deeply drifted, this narrow passage involves sparking dangerously up rock ribs and grooves – steep, loose and unprotected. Safer grooves and chockstones then lead quickly to the final obstacle, a direct corner exit, where the ascent degenerates into a struggle with greasy chockstones and some optimistic front-pointing up frozen earth.

# 75: AARDVARK (HVS) 85m

**Summary:** Spirited climbing up the grooved and overlapping arête of a remote mountain crag. Excellent rock. Good protection from careful use of double ropes.

**First Ascent:** M. Boysen, A. Williams and D. Little, 1966.

**Best Conditions:** The crag faces east at an altitude of 600m. Grass and lichen retard drying, although open face climbing on Aardvark is less affected. When dry the rock affords reassuring friction.

**Approach:** Access to the Aran area remains an extremely sensitive issue. It is important to approach only along recognised routes. Turn off the A494 Bala to Dolgellau road on the B4403 to Llanuwchllyn. Park at a lay-by 1km from the junction at GR.880 297. Follow the well-marked Aran Ridge path south for about 4km. The crag lies on the east side of the ridge above Llyn Lliwbran. Descend the broken hillside before reaching the crag and contour across to the area of arêtes and corners on its right-hand side. Refer to Outlying Areas map for general location, and map opposite for line of approach. GR.873 256. 1hr 30mins.

**Starting Point:** Scramble up grass to a ledge below and to the left of the niche. Refer to diagram.

**Descent:** Return along the ridge, or descend the Sloose corner with two long abseils.

Dry lichen crumbles under each wayward dab and grab from the proper route. Bubbly rock, rough as the contents of a Moelwyn pocket, lends support just the same. On a fine morning you could wander anywhere, it seems, on the sunlit pillars of Gist Ddu.

But it's not always like that. Entry to a sunless little niche at the beginning of the first pitch threatens to spoil the adventure before it has properly begun. To be fair there are compensations: a thread protects its undercut entry, and an *in situ* peg its rounded exit.

Easy slabs above the half-way terrace are no preparation for the overhang which follows. Fluttering beneath its eaves, supposedly building courage, merely drains stamina; the important thing is to get out left and over as quickly as possible so as to arrive strong and composed below the crucial bulge. Here an outstretched hand, painted with veins, touches a tiny flake. Fingertips curl, lock, pull. Lips draw back, caught between exultant exclamation and the scream. Success is in the balance.

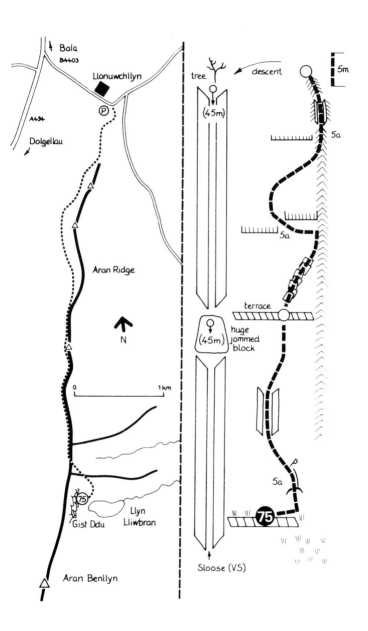

Bala
B4403

Llanuwchllyn

A494

Dolgellau

Aran Ridge

N

0          1 km

Gist Ddu          Llyn
                  Lliwbran

Aran Benllyn

tree          descent

(45m)

(45m)          huge
               jammed
               block

terrace

5m

5a

5a

5a

Sloose (VS)

# 76: ACHERON (VS+) 150m

**Summary:** A great adventure on the gloomy North Buttress of Cywarch, weaving a tortuous line up its imposing central rib. Solid but worryingly sharp rock (double ropes advisable!). Protection merely adequate.

**First Ascent:** A. J. J. Moulam and R. E. Lambe, May 1956.

**Best Conditions:** The buttress faces north-east at an altitude of 500m and dries slowly.

**Approach:** From Dinas Mawddwy. Refer to Outlying Areas map for general location. The road into Cwm Cywarch eventually crosses a cattle grid; park on grass at the far side of the meadow, where a track bears off left. Follow the signposted track to a foot-bridge over a stream below the North Buttress. Refer to Route 77 map for details. GR.848 196. 30mins.

**Starting Point:** From the foot-bridge note the clean, light coloured rib just left of centre on the big buttress directly above. Start on a grass ledge between the rib and a large corner to its right (Doom, VS).

**Descent:** Either along the ramp which slants down to the right of the buttress, or continue upwards and descend well to the right of the crag.

The first touch is disappointing. Sharp-edged rock cuts into fingers and boot soles but lacks the rough texture of Gist Ddu. Moss, lichen and lack of protection add to the unpleasantness and insecurity. A sudden overlap, gymnastic and protected, promises better things to come.

A grooved rib forces a long and poorly waymarked diversion to the right; first across an exposed wall and nose, then back across slabs to a groove of shattered spikes – a mixture of worry and comfort. The rib sharpens, bulges and puts an end to it. Huge holds on the leftward escape are good defence against the second's abusive remarks about lack of protection.

A semi-hand traverse across razor flakes recovers the rib line. You can hear the leader chuckling while fixing the belay at its end; an astute choice of pitches has swung the pitches his way – the crux comes next. It looks simple, this slanting little chimney. But what an effort of bridging! Its frictionless slabby half soon lays back into a ramp but there is no rest, no respite, no runner. Only the handholds offer encouragement. The second sniggers, deceived by appearances. His time will come.

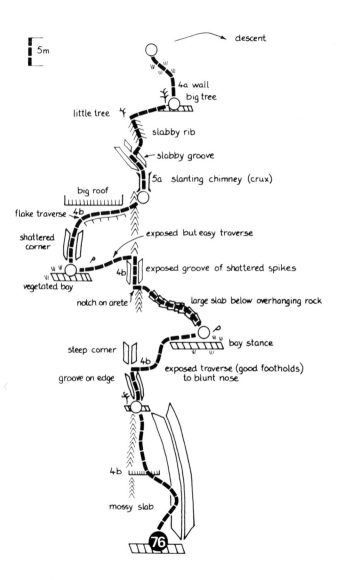

descent

4a wall
big tree

little tree

slabby rib

slabby groove

5a slanting chimney (crux)

big roof

flake traverse 4b

exposed but easy traverse

shattered corner

exposed groove of shattered spikes

vegetated bay

4b

notch on arete

large slab below overhanging rock

bay stance

steep corner

4b

exposed traverse (good footholds) to blunt nose

groove on edge

4b

mossy slab

76

# 77: MAESGLASAU FALLS (IV) 225m

**Summary:** A magnificent ice climb up the head wall of a secluded valley. Its central section can form as a great tumbling ice-fall, 100m high and 25m wide. Mainly screw protection and belays.

**First Ascent:** J. Sumner and G. Kirkham, February 1979.

**Best Conditions:** North-east facing at an altitude of less than 500m. The falls drain an extensive area of boggy upland, which accounts for the huge build-up of ice after many days of intense cold. Reaches optimum condition only during the very best seasons.

**Approach:** From the A470 Dolgellau to Dinas Mawddwy road (parking on verge). Follow the track and footpath on the south-east side of the valley. Finally, contour rightwards across the head of the cwm. Ascend a vegetated rib, left of the lower gully, until an exposed ledge traverses into the ice-fall. Refer to Outlying Areas map for general location, and map opposite for details of approach. GR.828 141. 1hr.

**Starting Point:** In a bay below the first main fall.

**Descent:** Continue up the hillside above and descend the ridge path leftwards, rejoining the approach path where it begins to contour the head of the cwm.

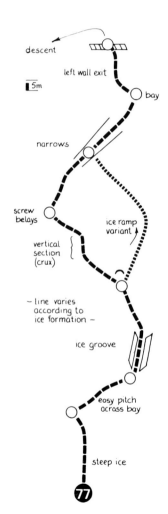

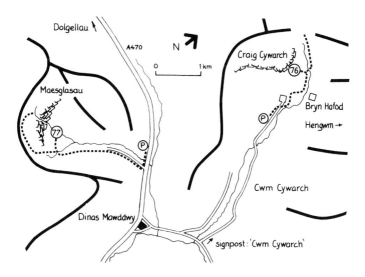

Ice climbing in Wales has little to do with snow and mountains. Instead the essential ingredients are an infinite supply of bog drainage and a barrier cliff. Now leave to stand, at minus ten degrees, for the proverbial forty days and forty nights. Thaw for twelve hours before serving. The kids love it.

Rural Maesglasau is a most unlikely setting for a major winter expedition. The fall can be seen from the main road several kilometres distant. It takes the breath away.

An introductory pitch oils the clockwork claws, but does little to prepare you psychologically for what follows. Height estimates of the main fall can be wildly inaccurate; only when the rope runs out in the middle of nowhere does the true scale become apparent. Ice umbrellas block the direct continuation. Some will creep beneath them up to the right, while others will cross the main fall diagonally leftwards to a belay on screws – an unprecedented second consecutive stance on ice. Above the main fall a miniature gully twists the route through narrowing walls to its terminus in a bay below the head wall. A final pitch exits into an alien world, safe and flat.

# Coastal Areas

Routes selected for this section have been drawn from two locations: the roadside outcrops at Tremadog, and the cluster of sea cliffs around Gogarth bay on Anglesey. Development of both areas began much later than elsewhere – in the fifties at Tremadog, and in the sixties at Gogarth. At one time both locations were used primarily as wet weather or winter alternatives to the mountain crags. However, it soon became evident that the quality of climbing was at least as good as anything in central areas.

Gogarth intimidates first-time visitors. Added complications of abseil or tidal approaches undermine confidence already rattled by the lurking sea, collapsing approach ledges, and unrelieved verticality. Contrasts between Wen Zawn, the Main Cliff, Upper Tier and South Stack are staggering. Strand, for instance, a conventional *E1* on the Upper Tier, yields an entirely different climbing experience to that of Mousetrap, also *E1*, on the appalling rock of South Stack. This meagre selection can only hint at the tremendous scope.

Tremadog is more friendly. The routes here are sunny, accessible, and almost without exception on superb rock. From a technical point of view they are among the finest in Britain. A lowland setting completes the outcrop atmosphere.

**Approaches:** Tremadog can be reached in half an hour's drive from the Llanberis Pass or Ogwen. Refer to Outlying Areas map for details. Gogarth is a little further away, although the approach via the A5 from Bangor to Holyhead is relatively fast. Daily travel using public transport is not very practical. However, for longer periods of stay the train service between Bangor and Holyhead could be useful. Tremadog is slightly more accessible. Buses run from Caernarfon and Beddgelert, while Porthmadog (a few kilometres from Tremadog) is served by the Barmouth rail line.

**Accommodation and Services:** Refer also to listings under main area headings.

Gogarth: *Camping*, unofficial, near South Stack; café at South Stack; other accommodation and services in Holyhead.

Tremadog: *Camping*, ideally situated site, barn (and café) at Bwlch y Moch; other services in Tremadog and Porthmadog.

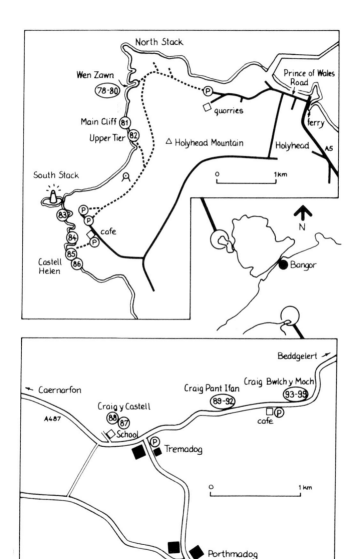

*The Strand (Route 82), Gogarth Upper Tier.*

*The crucial traverse on Hardd (Route 100), Carreg Hylldrem.*

# 78: BRITOMARTIS (VS+) & SPIDER WALL (HVS) 60m

**Summary:** Exhilarating climbing above a waiting sea. Both routes ascend the vertical wall above Spider's Web arch on good holds. Intricate route finding on Spider Wall. Mostly good protection. Abseil approach.

**First Ascent:** Britomartis – D. Alcock and G. Rogan, February 1967; Spider Wall – L. E. Holliwell, D. S. Potts and L. R. Holliwell, June 1969.

**Best Conditions:** Faces north-west but dries quickly. Not normally tidal, although waves carried by a high tide could break over the starting ledge during rough weather (tide tables available from stationers in Holyhead).

**Approach:** Via Holyhead Quarries. Refer to Coastal Areas map for details. From the parking area follow the uphill track, and later fork left to stay on the main track. The path divides again; take the left fork (main track again) to a shallow col. Descend a grass couloir on the far side. 20mins.

**Starting Point:** Descend to a promontory with fine but frightening views of Wen Slab. A deep fissure at its seaward end indicates the exit of the Trap chimney. Abseil 40m down the chimney line to a large ledge. Ropes could easily jam during retrieval so it is worth bringing an extra rope to leave in place.

Sea cliff climbing is the most absurd branch of mountaineering. Who can rationalise abseiling *down* in order to begin climbing *up*? It can only happen because the flatlands of Anglesey sever the link between climber and mountain. On arrival at Holy Island his head is filled with the fascination of the sea, therefore the paradox does not arise and the abseil proceeds.

A bridging rest across a groove restores balance after the initial, finger-flake traverse. Its continuation, the crack line of Britomartis, beckons with huge layaway holds. But to follow Spider Wall you must tear yourself away and set off on a devious diagonal above the arch – rock and runners above, sea and seals below. Nothing is obvious; promising fracture lines break off in all directions, only to fizzle out after a few moves. Intuition (or could it be trial and error?) eventually singles out the true line. The slow art of the wall climber – the searching, reaching, testing, and pulling – finds its ideal subject in Spider Wall.

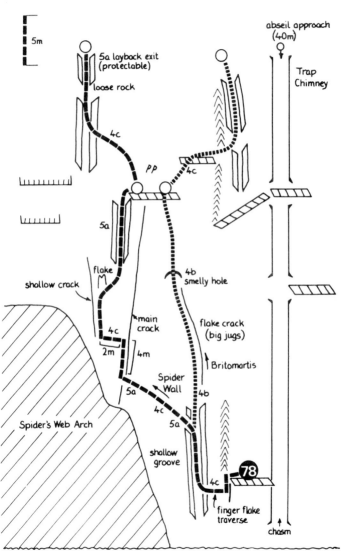

5m

abseil approach (40m)

Trap Chimney

5a layback exit (protectable)

loose rock

4c

P P

4c

5a

4b smelly hole

flake

shallow crack

main crack

flake crack (big jugs)

4c

2m

4m

Britomartis

Spider Wall

5a

4c

4b

Spider's Web Arch

5a

shallow groove

78

4c

finger flake traverse

chasm

the sea, the sea

# 79: A DREAM OF WHITE HORSES (HVS) 120m

**Summary:** A Gogarth classic, internationally famous and the epitome of sea cliff climbing in Wales. Girdles Wen Zawn from right to left with unexpected technical ease. Unusually serious, with little protection on the first pitch, and no means of escape from the last.

**First Ascent:** E. Drummond and D. Pearce, October 1968.

**Best Conditions:** Faces northwest but dries quickly. A good climb for a calm, sunny afternoon in spring or autumn. Non-tidal by the described start.

**Approach:** Via Holyhead Quarries, as for Route 78. A popular traversing start avoids the abseil approach to sea-level and maintains the logic of the route. First descend to the promontory opposite Wen Slab to identify the approach gully and entry notch (unfortunately the route looks horrific from here so the attempt may proceed no further than this!). When ready, traverse across the cliff top and scramble carefully down the gully (for future reference note the obvious abseil block on the edge of the slab, about half-way down).

**Starting Point:** At the previously identified notch and scoop on the right-hand side of the slab.

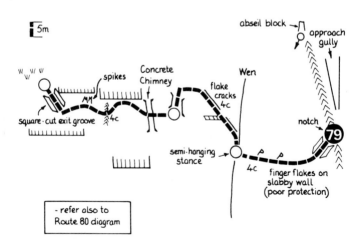

- refer also to
Route 80 diagram

A Dream of White Horses risks being overtaken by its classic reputation. There was a time, not so very long ago, when only a select few knew of its secret, while the rest stood awestruck on the promontory, belittled by its *Extreme* grade and improbable line across the back wall of the Zawn. Leo Dickinson encapsulated their worst fears in his first ascent photograph of Drummond and Pearce creeping, ant-like, across the slab, while the spray from thundering white horses spattered the rock beneath their feet. Since then the word has got around. Now everyone knows Dream is a soft touch at *HVS*. Provided you can keep your head. But who can? No one is immune to the mental battering doled out by Wen Zawn. Stormy or calm, you grow dizzy from the creeping fear that some great disaster is about to befall you. It is a symptom of the Gogarth disease, which has no known cure.

Slabs are rare on Gogarth. This explains why the wall of the first pitch is called a slab. To be fair the climbing does involve balancing across on little incuts and flatties, so perhaps the core of the definition is satisfied (the lack of protection is certainly consistent with the type). Compared to this a hanging stance in the wide crack of Wen, supported by the two-dozen unused nuts on your rack, seems quite secure.

Diagonal flake cracks, energetic and protected, restore some degree of normality to the climb. Had they been aligned horizontally then the pitch would be little more than an exposed seaside stroll. As it is, their upward tilt maintains a comfortable handrail, while at the same time withdrawing proper foot support. The net effect is equivalent to climbing a hand traverse that has been propped up on its end.

The crossing of Concrete Chimney, that curious rubble-filled rift, signals entry into a very different terrain. Yellow rock, rattling teeth, tottering spikes – this is more like South Stack than Wen Zawn. Undercut by the sea, its mortared joints in poor state of repair, this back wall of the zawn is poised in a state of unstable equilibrium. The bit beneath your feet went some time ago, while the overhang above your head is about ready to shove off. It makes for exciting climbing. Incidentally, do you know how to prusik?

# 80: WEN (VS+) & CONCRETE CHIMNEY (HVS) 80m

**Summary:** Big, atmospheric routes up the main face of Wen Zawn. Technically reasonable climbing in a serious setting. Good protection on Wen, adequate on Concrete Chimney. Abseil approach.

**First Ascent:** Wen – J. Brown and M. Boysen, May 1966; Concrete Chimney – P. Crew and J. Brown, February 1967.

**Best Conditions:** As for Route 79. An optional entry pitch to Wen is tidal, and even when clear may be affected by spray or drainage (tide tables available from shops in Holyhead). In truly stormy weather the spray from breaking waves can easily reach the Wen Ledges, 30m above the sea!

**Approach:** As for Route 79 to the abseil block in the gully right of Wen Slab. Make a 40m diagonal abseil down and left on to the Wen Ledges (ideally use an extra rope which can be recovered later). Traverse the ledges leftwards to gain the crack line of Wen. At low tide, make a second abseil from here to ledges at sea-level below the initial chimney of Wen (this increases the standard of Wen to borderline *HVS*).

High tide or low, the greasy entry pitch to Wen could be ignored and a start made from ledges reached after the first abseil. However, the temptation is always to make the second abseil to sea-level and include a chimney which, in technical terms, provides the finest climbing on the route. A tough decision, because there is no going back after pulling down those ropes.

The main crack presents few difficulties, provided you can learn to live with a colony of suicidal miniature scorpions, whose members leap from the crack each time you disturb their habitat with a sinking jam or nut runner (which on Wen is pretty often). Don Whillans disappointed viewers of a BBC outside broadcast by romping up this pitch, declaring it 'easy' and complaining about the surfeit of 'bloody big jugs'. The top pitch demands more respect, but they didn't show that on the telly.

Concrete Chimney blends elegant climbing into the Wen atmosphere to produce a sequence of exquisite moves up the steepening left edge of the slab. The Concrete Chimney itself, a geological freak, is exactly that. No one in their right mind would want to climb this solidified dribble so pinch your nose, tiptoe across, and finish ecstatically up the Dream head wall.

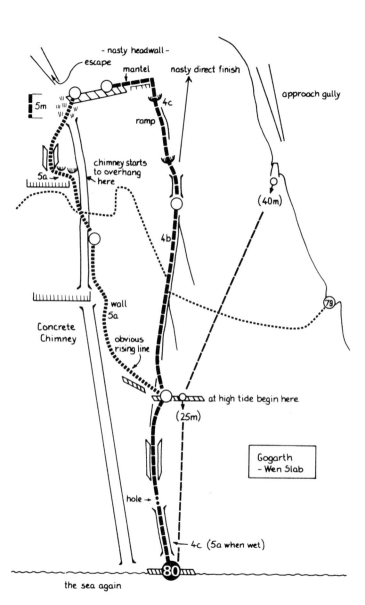

# 81: GOGARTH (E1) 110m

**Summary:** A demanding route in every respect up the right edge of the most impressive sea cliff in Wales. Varied climbing, spacious stances, adequate protection.

**First Ascent:** B. Ingle and M. Boysen, April 1964.

**Best Conditions:** The cliff faces west and dries relatively quickly. Climbable during all but the coldest weather. Non-tidal approach.

**Approach:** Via South Stack. Refer to Coastal Areas map for details. Follow paths inland, passing the two radio stations, towards Holyhead Mountain. The path divides; follow the left branch, descending gradually, to a platform above the approach gully. Awesome views of the Main Cliff. 25mins.

**Starting Point:** Scramble down the gully and descend left to boulders at sea-level. Cross slabs to sloping ledges below the prominent corner of Emulator. Continue left then climb down easily to a crack on the right side of Gogarth Pinnacle.

**Descent:** Walk rightwards along the cliff top, then scramble down a short chimney and slabs to the platform above the approach gully (if in doubt, descend well to the right of all cliffs).

Gogarth Pinnacle spans the frontier between Upper Tier and Main Cliff, between coastal outcrop and true sea cliff. Here the sea enhances the quality of the climbing, without dictating terms.

An easy jamming crack gets the climb under way (not many of those at Gogarth so make the most of it). A sunny perch on top of the Pinnacle bestows calm and contentment. See the inquisitive seals and furious gulls; feel the sunlight burning into boot-cramped toes; listen to the thump and hiss of breaking waves . . .

Wake up, you've done nothing yet. The wall traverse calls for a leader with guts, or failing that one with iron arms and a slick technique with wire runners. A hidden groove beyond adds to the growing sense of unease. Relax; two easier pitches follow, the second of which – a slanting corner crack – proves to be the finest (and easiest) of the route.

Previously the route was graded *HVS*, despite *Extreme* climbing on the top pitch. Perhaps it will seem straightforward when approached as an *E1*. Let's hope so. A devious traverse gains the crux – a crack begun on poor jams and completed on strenuous layaways. A half rest and spike runner arrive when it's all over. Typical Gogarth.

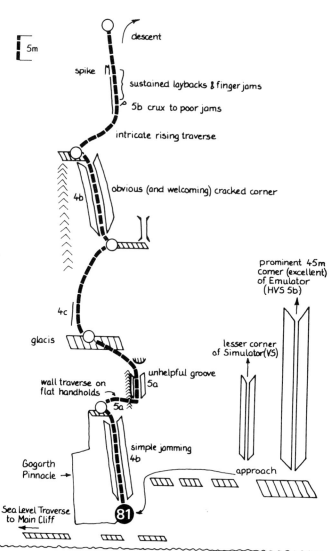

descent

5m

spike

sustained laybacks & finger jams

5b crux to poor jams

intricate rising traverse

4b

obvious (and welcoming) cracked corner

4c

glacis

prominent 45m corner (excellent) of Emulator (HVS 5b)

lesser corner of Simulator (VS)

unhelpful groove 5a

wall traverse on flat handholds

5a

Gogarth Pinnacle

simple jamming 4b

approach

81

Sea Level Traverse to Main Cliff

more sea

# 82: CENTRAL PARK (VS+) & THE STRAND (E1) 60m

**Summary:** Popular climbs on Central Park Wall, a compact facet of the Upper Tier. Central Park adopts a circuitous and serious approach to a strenuous but safe crack. Strand climbs directly up an elegant and well-protected face crack at the upper limit of its grade.

**First Ascent:** Central Park – P. Crew and D. Alcock, May 1966; The Strand – E. Drummond (unseconded), October 1967.

**Best Conditions:** The wall faces north-west but dries relatively quickly. Climbable at any time of year; although the shady aspect, and fingery climbing, rule out cold winter days. Non-tidal approach.

**Approach:** As for Route 81 to the bottom of the approach gully. Follow a decaying traverse path beneath the Upper Tier, across a tricky rock traverse, to a ledge below the wall (confirm location by identifying Shag Rock, a 25m pinnacle at the right-hand side of the wall).

**Starting Point:** Refer to diagram.

**Descent:** Scramble up steep grass above the wall and walk rightwards along the cliff top. Scramble down a short chimney and slabs to the platform above the approach gully (if in doubt descend well to the right of all cliffs).

Climbing on the Upper Tier is supposed to lack the seriousness of that on 'proper' sea cliffs. Survivors of the collapsing approach and aimless first pitch of Central Park would disagree. Eventually the route stumbles upon a wide crack which promises good protection and sinking jams, and shows good sense by following it without deviation to the top.

Once, the routes on this wall cut obvious trails through a vertical pasture of sea grass. Nowadays, criss-crossed by eliminates, Central Park Wall is fast becoming a trackless desert. For all that, the line of Strand remains unmistakable as a single, soaring crack line creased at intervals by lesser diagonals.

Holds on Strand improve in direct proportion to the steepening angle. From this you will deduce, correctly, that somewhere in the middle is a steepish wall of poorish holds. Protection is potentially good, but trying to place it all invites failure. Since no one move can be singled out as the crux, a more successful strategy is to climb confidently for several metres beyond protection until the next good rest point. It's all in the mind.

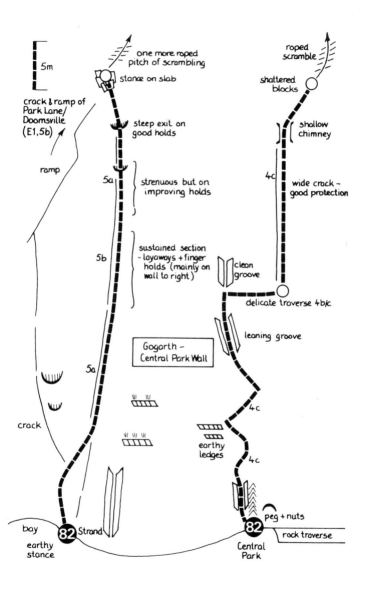

5m

crack & ramp of
Park Lane/
Doomsville
(E1,5b)

ramp

one more roped
pitch of scrambling

stance on slab

steep exit on
good holds

5a          strenuous but on
            improving holds

5b          sustained section
            - layaways + finger
            holds (mainly on
            wall to right)

Gogarth –
Central Park Wall

5a

crack

bay
earthy
stance

82  Strand

roped
scramble

shattered
blocks

shallow
chimney

4c          wide crack –
            good protection

clean
groove

delicate traverse 4b/c

leaning groove

4c

4c
earthy
ledges

4c

peg + nuts

82  Central
    Park

rock traverse

# 83: MOUSETRAP (E1) 130m

**Summary:** Bizarre climbing among preferentially weathered troughs of solidified mud. Technically reasonable but unusually serious. Poor protection, untrustworthy rock. Abseil approach.

**First Ascent:** J. Brown and P. Crew, October 1966.

**Best Conditions:** Faces south-west and dries quickly. Suitable for cold weather. A voluntary ban on climbing operates in Mousetrap Zawn from 1 February to 31 July each year to protect nesting birds (updated information on notice boards above the cliffs).

**Approach:** From Holyhead to South Stack car-park immediately above Mousetrap Zawn. Refer to Coastal Areas map for details. Cross the cliff-top wall and descend grass to a block above the promontory between Mousetrap Zawn and Left-Hand Red Wall (refer to Route 84 crag diagram). Tie two 45m ropes together and abseil down the promontory to boulder fields in the zawn floor. Alternatively, at low tide, approach from the lighthouse steps (tide tables available in Holyhead).

**Starting Point:** Below a groove, left of the cave mouth.

Students of geology marvel at the convoluted structure of Mousetrap Zawn. As climbers, we may lack their sophisticated terminology but we know a heap of tot when we see one. The wall looks like a wormery, a ploughed field, a squashed pile of salami sarnies – anything but a rock face fit for climbing. A hands-on inspection from the zawn floor does nothing to change this view.

The climbing is easy at first; but a traverse into curving chimneys, soon after, surely asks too much from this ephemeral medium. A high side runner and persuasive second (who has one eye on the incoming tide) overrule objections. After a full rope length of stop-go progress you arrive, nerves shattered, on a large sloping ledge above the cave.

A frothy wall above the ledge leads into a chimney grown dusty with neglect since Crew mistakenly wormed up it during the first ascent. To its right, the knobs of harder red rock protrude like chicken heads – ignore the squawks of protest and get going.

A red wall on the final pitch guards exit from the face. In purely technical terms this is the crux, although its frequent runners and semi-permanent holds must surely be worth a discount of ten per cent – which is ten per cent more than you'll get from the ice-cream man at the top stance. Weird.

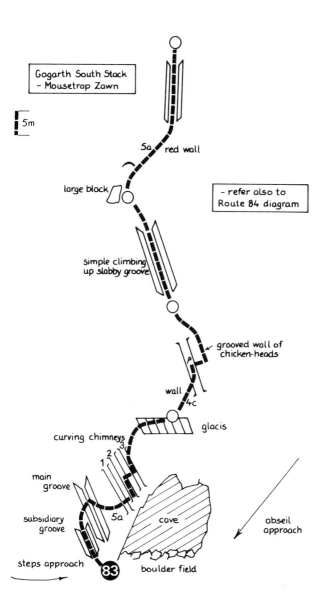

Gogarth South Stack
– Mousetrap Zawn

5m

5a   red wall

large block

simple climbing
up slabby groove

– refer also to
Route 84 diagram

grooved wall of
chicken-heads

P

wall
4c

glacis

curving chimneys

2  3
1

main
groove

5a

subsidiary
groove

cove

abseil
approach

steps approach

83

boulder field

# 84: RED WALL (E1) 80m

**Summary:** Ugly but morbidly fascinating climbing in a tremendous situation. Technically more demanding than Mousetrap (Route 83), but on slightly better rock. Abseil approach.

**First Ascent:** J. Brown and P. Crew, September 1966.

**Best Conditions:** Faces southwest and dries quickly. Suitable for cold weather. The ridge approach is feasible only at low water (tide tables available in Holyhead). A voluntary ban on climbing operates on Red Wall from 1 February to 31 July each year to protect nesting birds (updated information on notice boards above the cliffs).

**Approach:** From Holyhead to the car-park at South Stack Café. Refer to Coastal Areas map for details. At low tide, abseil down the ridge opposite Red Wall. Make a second abseil to boulders at sea-level in the gulch between ridge and wall. Finally, scramble nervously up rock and mud to the foot of the wall. Alternatively, abseil down the wall on 60m of fixed rope (having previously formulated a strategy for passing the knot!).

**Starting Point:** On a block stance below the wall.

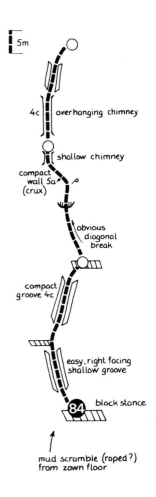

5m

4c | overhanging chimney

shallow chimney

compact wall 5a (crux)

obvious diagonal break

compact groove 4c

easy, right facing shallow groove

**84** block stance

mud scramble (roped?) from zawn floor

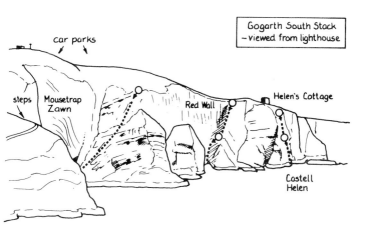

Whatever possessed Brown and Crew to set off up this wall? From the viewpoint above Castell Helen it looks appalling – sixty metres of runny red and yellow rock resting on a heap of mud. Nesting birds seem to find it attractive, but *climbers*?

Few approaches are as unpleasant as this – an abseiling descent into a black, slimy pit where the snaking tongues of a rising tide lick and slurp at debris fallen from the face. The sole means of escape is a precarious scrabble up a mud slope into the comparative safety of the wall. Attractive? It's beautiful!

Joe Brown recollects that during the first ascent the holds were 'so thin and big they snapped off like biscuits'. From his description you can accurately predict the most effective technique for climbing Red Wall: mould your body into the erosion holes, bridge and pinch to help distribute the load, breathe softly, and speak quietly. Protection from slings draped over petrified chicken heads is illusory, but it does help to shed weight that might otherwise overload the footholds. The paradox is that this whole experience is compelling to the point of intoxication. Ice climbers will understand.

# 85: BLANCO (HVS) 70m

**Summary:** Exciting climbing on surprisingly good rock up the front face of Castell Helen, the most conventional of South Stack cliffs. A popular introduction to Gogarth, but not one to be underestimated. Abseil approach.

**First Ascent:** J. Brown and D. Alcock, September 1966.

**Best Conditions:** Faces south-west and dries quickly. Climbable at any time of year provided the approach traverse is not threatened by waves.

**Approach:** From Holyhead to the car-park at South Stack Café. Refer to Coastal Areas map for details. Approach the cliff top via Helen's Cottage. Abseil from a metal spike (back-ups advisable) to a platform half-way down the wall. A second abseil from the right end of the platform leads down Atlantis groove to ledges just above the sea. Take care not to let ropes fall into the sea during retrieval (risk of jamming). Ideally use a spare rope, at least for the first abseil.

**Starting Point:** Move left from the groove to gain ledges on the front face. Traverse these to a niche below a crack and groove line which leads up to the left end of the half-way platform.

South Stack could be the edge of the world. Solid earth beneath your feet continually reassures, but you can never fully escape the irrational fear of toppling into that great void to seaward.

Climbers sit quietly in South Stack Café, guidebooks unopened before them while they sip tea to delay departure. Finally summoned they creep outside into a scene bleached of colour by the pale sky and white rock. Abseil rigging concentrates their thoughts for a few moments, but soon the waves of vertigo begin washing over them.

The first abseil to the platform cuts across every instinct. Screeching gulls, frothing sea, inaccessible ledge: this is the stuff of childhood nightmares – stranded on a hidden ledge above the sea, screams drowned by crashing waves, parents walking away to mourn their lost child.

The idea of sea cliff climbing seems much less terrifying once you actually get down to sea-level. Could this be aversion therapy in action? Whatever the explanation, the second abseil to ledges just above the sea restores rational hopes and fears. Ropes uncoiled, runners racked, a cliff to climb: this is the old, familiar story. Now all you have to do is climb the route.

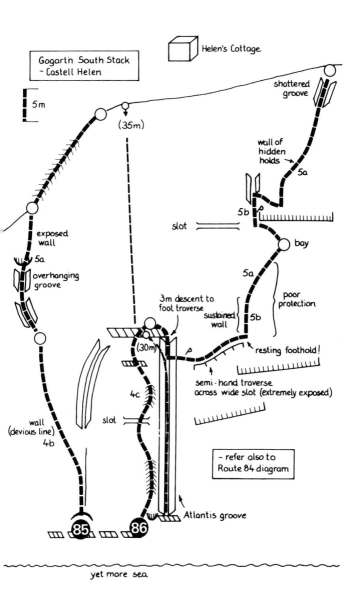

Helen's Cottage

Gogarth South Stack
~ Castell Helen

5m

(35m)

shattered
groove

wall of
hidden
holds

5a

5b

slot

exposed
wall

5a

overhanging
groove

bay

5a

poor
protection

5b

3m descent to
fool traverse

sustained
wall

resting foothold!

(30m)

semi-hand traverse
across wide slot (extremely exposed)

4c

slot

wall
(devious line)
4b

- refer also to
Route 84 diagram

85    86    Atlantis groove

yet more sea

# 86: TRUE MOMENTS/FREEBIRD (E2) 95m

**Summary:** Devious and difficult climbing in a tremendous position above the sea. Climbs the undercut red wall on the right-hand side of Castell Helen by linking a series of horizontal faults. Needs cunning to protect properly. Abseil approach. Illustrated on Route 85 diagram.

**First Ascent:** True Moments – A. Hyslop and D. Knighton, May 1978; Freebird – A. Evans, N. Siddiqui, G. Milburn and J. Moran, March 1978.

**Best Conditions:** Faces south-west, and dries quickly apart from a few isolated drainage streaks. Climbable at any time of year, provided waves are not breaking over the starting ledges.

**Approach:** As for Route 85 to ledges at the bottom of Atlantis groove.

**Starting Point:** On the first usable ledge after traversing out of Atlantis, just left of the undercut right edge of the front face.

Flared cracks in the sea-scoured lower wall of Castell Helen spit out runners faster than you can place them. This could be a worry but for the ladder of holds set into solid grey rock. Aim to arrive refreshed and exhilarated on the half-way platform – or risk being repulsed by the second and crucial pitch.

From three metres down Atlantis groove a rising fault line cuts across the face – an open invitation to the bold or brainless. The position is extremely exposed. After an initial few moves of feet shuffling there is no alternative but to drop down and begin hand traversing the fault towards a distant foothold rest. The second watches intently from the platform, and hopes the leader will remember to leave one rope free for a high runner. But the leader has other concerns. Having stood up above the slot he contemplates five metres of sustained climbing on flat finger holds with little immediate prospect of a runner. Ropes hang beneath in a limp catenary, minimising drag but increasing the potential fall. Gradually, the climbing eases to an uncomfortable stance below the top overhang. A move over it on to the top wall proves as technical as anything previously encountered, although a peg runner and nearby second help relieve the tension. True Moments finishes directly, while Freebird lingers, squeezing extra moments from an unlikely sequence across the head wall. A perfect setting for the final act.

# 87: TENSOR (HVS) 70m & THE WASP (E1) 55m

**Summary:** Excellent climbing on good rock among the grooves and overlaps of a compact lowland outcrop. Both pitches on Wasp are strenuous and sustained, although the main difficulties are well protected. On Tensor, isolated difficult moves – often in spectacular situations – punctuate stretches of easier climbing. Illustrated on Route 88 diagram.

**First Ascent:** Tensor – J. Brown and C. E. Davies, March 1964; The Wasp – J. Brown and C. E. Davies, September 1960.

**Best Conditions:** Faces south-west at low altitude and dries quickly after rain. After prolonged bad weather drainage may affect the cracks and overlaps of both routes for a day or two. Climbable at any time of year.

**Approach:** As for Route 88.

**Starting Point:** At the foot of a large slab on the right-hand side of the central nose.

**Descent:** As for Route 88.

An upward view of the face foreshortens the slabby walls of Tensor to reveal only the underside of its huge overhangs. Those already at work appear to be weaving impossible lines through and over them, their ropes hung in loops beneath, swaying. This is not an encouraging sight.

Photographers have chosen to portray Tensor as a layback entry to a hanging groove. In fact this compositional crux passes uneventfully. The real crux comes later – at a teetering exit to pegs beneath the top roof. The roof itself usually succumbs to a thrash and grab from aid slings, less often from noble free attempts.

Wasp discourages casual attempts with fifteen metres of gently overhanging crack. Runners protect every move, but sooner or later you must abandon yourself to the gritstone climber's ethos and make a bid for the top. The aid slings and ivy roots have long gone from its exit, but there's a finishing jug if you can hang on long enough to find it.

A spacious belay ledge upsets the continuity of the climbing, so that starting the top groove becomes a struggle to regain lost momentum. Once entered there is no respite; three metres of precarious friction climbing precede easier but equally sustained bridging to a buzzing back-and-foot exit.

# 88: CREAGH DHU WALL (S+) 60m

**Summary:** A route of outstanding quality up the central nose of a pleasantly situated lowland outcrop. Varied and unusual climbing help to make this one of the most attractive climbs at Tremadog. Adequate protection, idyllic stances. Double ropes recommended.

**First Ascent:** J. Cunningham, W. Smith and P. Vaughan, July 1951.

**Best Conditions:** Faces west at low altitude and dries very quickly after rain. Climbable at any time of year.

**Approach:** From Tremadog village on the A498 (parking at the T-junction). Then, 400m west of the T-junction, turn right, along the school lane. Continue along a track past the school and then turn right to follow a path, adjacent to a fenced wall, across fields. Turn right at the trees and then left soon after, to ascend boulder slopes to the foot of the crag. Refer to Outlying Areas map for general location, and Coastal Areas map for details. GR.558 403. 20mins.

**Starting Point:** At a large block below the central nose, a few metres up to the left from where the main approach path arrives at the crag.

**Descent:** Traverse rightwards, just above the top of the main face, to enter and descend a gully among trees. Some of this is quite tricky.

At the first stance a long-suffering tree propels eager leaders into the first cracked groove. Hearts flutter at a brief layback, but more through excited anticipation than the fear of falling. Already the route exudes quality.

An inferior direct variant exits direct from the niche, while the original peeps out right to discover the toe traverse. This single thin foothold extends almost to the far side of the slab; a controlled fall for handholds makes good the final deficiency. Stout trees above secure the finest stance at Tremadog.

A hand traverse returns you to the nose, where a final skidding pull on to a spike brings gasps of relief. Zigzagging moves up the wall sustain the exposure wonderfully, while a substantial mantelshelf hereabouts turns out be the top stance! From here the original finish goes up left, entering a polished scoop with a hard move and nearby runner. A fine Direct Finish has better friction and is technically no more difficult. Unfortunately, the protection is terrible. Your choice.

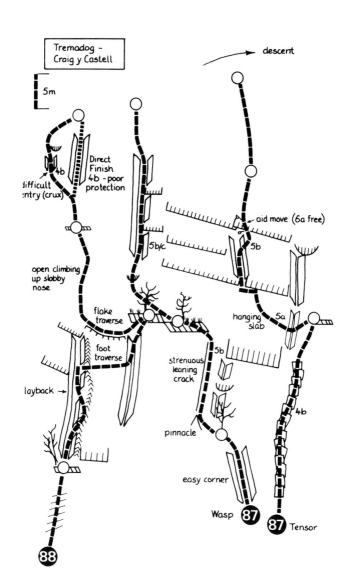

Tremadog –
Craig y Castell

5m

descent

Direct
Finish
4b – poor
protection

difficult
entry (crux)

4b

open climbing
up slobby
nose

aid move (6a free)

5b

5b/c

flake
traverse

hanging
slab

5a

foot
traverse

5b

strenuous
leaning
crack

layback

pinnacle

4b

easy corner

Wasp **87**

**87** Tensor

**88**

# 89: BORCHGREVINCK/POOR MAN'S PEUTEREY (S+) 70m

**Summary:** A fascinating route, adventurous and varied. One of the best at this grade in Wales. Requires cunning to protect properly. Double ropes useful.

**First Ascent:** Borchgrevinck – C. T. Jones and J. R. Sims, April 1957; Poor Man's Peuterey – G. J. Sutton and J. Gaukroger, December 1953.

**Best Conditions:** Faces south at low altitude and dries quickly (although the first pitch can be greasy in winter).

**Approach:** Periodic rock falls at Pant Ifan place landowners in a difficult legal position. Notices try to discourage climbing.

Approach from Bwlch y Moch Café on the A498 Beddgelert to Tremadog road (large parking area). The crag is obvious from here, high up on the left skyline. Cross the stile a few hundred metres west and go up a boulder field and winding path. A 2m rock step in the path below the crag is a good landmark. Refer to Outlying Areas map for general location and Coastal Areas map for details. GR.571 407. 15mins.

**Starting Point:** Descend the step and continue up left for about 40m. Traverse rightwards over disintegrating ledges to a recess with unusual tree root above.

**Descent:** As for Route 91.

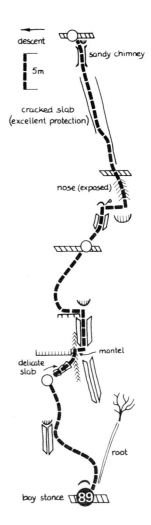

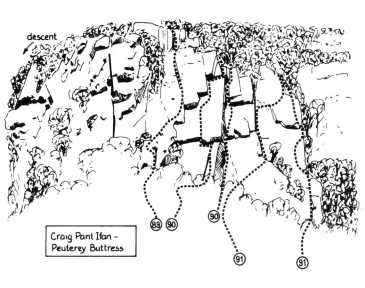

descent

Craig Pant Ifan –
Peuterey Buttress

Few crags are as attractive as Peuterey Buttress. Zigzag bands of overhangs isolate and emphasise its upper slabs, open and inviting above the trees. The rock is perfect.

Little of this is evident from the earthy ledge at its foot. Of more immediate concern is a balancy, rising traverse across the lower wall. It ends below a roof with no obvious means of continuation. Something to think about while belaying the rope.

A tree root once aided the tricky step up to the right, while an earth ledge caught the clumsy footed. Now both are gone to leave an exposed sequence of moves, culminating in an awkward semi-mantel at the right extremity of the roof. A hidden corner now reveals itself. It proves less helpful than first appearances suggest; a short but gutsy hand traverse puts it behind.

The luxurious midway ledge has gone too. Now the second must share the exposure, as the leader – fingers lingering on an ancient piton – tiptoes out on to the nose. An upper slab flows by in a swirl of protected crack climbing at gentle angles. A final sandy chimney – overhanging and unpleasant – pulls the plug.

# 90: PINCUSHION & BARBARIAN (HVS) 60m

**Summary:** Pincushion struggles over a roof – using one or two points of aid at this standard – to win the finest slab pitch at Tremadog. Slabs and overhangs also dominate the climbing on Barbarian, despite its big corner line. Good runners protect the main difficulties on both routes.

**First Ascent:** Pincushion (as an aid route) – D. P. Davies, M. J. Harris and R. R. E. Chorley, October 1956; Barbarian (as an aid route, later climbed free by J. Brown) – C. T. Jones, C. E. Davies, E. Millington and M. King, August 1958.

**Best Conditions:** Faces south at low altitude. The entry to Pincushion can be greasy, but the main pitch dries very quickly. Barbarian carries some drainage and takes longer to dry, when it becomes gritty (you can't win). Climbable at any time of year.

**Approach:** As for Route 89.

**Starting Point:** Barbarian: traverse ledges leftwards from above the rock step and climb a 5m wall (one tricky step) to a tree. Continue easily for another 5m to the foot of the big corner. Pincushion: in a small bay just right of Route 89.

**Descent:** As for Route 91.

Pincushion asserts itself in one big pitch. First make your second comfortable at the well-appointed tree stance (it will be a long wait). Now you may explore the chimney. Secreted in its smelly depths will be old nests, dropped slings and the other debris of ancient struggles. Thankfully, you need enter it fully only for the final few metres.

At the roof, a double sling drapes over a blunt spike (the launching platform for the crucial move on Silly Arête), as protection for antics to follow. A knee-and-foot jam across the chimney steadies the horrific stretch to clip the tat beneath the roof. Now close your eyes and slither across. If you peep over the roof the slab will now reveal its secret. Slot a runner, crank the fingers, and set off on the lead of your life.

Barbarian has its moments too. First, from a half-rest in a niche midway across the roof, arrange fingers and runners above the lip. Now wind yourself up into a spring, take a deep breath, and uncoil upwards into the groove. Finally, rope drag permitting, semi-mantel out left on to a tiny ledge. This in turn becomes the stance. Enjoy it; it may not be here for much longer.

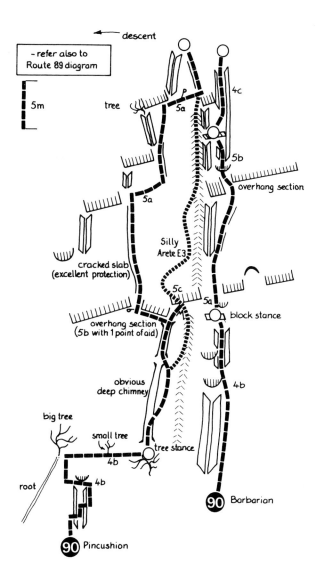

descent

- refer also to
Route 89 diagram

5m

tree

4c

5a

5b

overhang section

5a

Silly
Arete E3

cracked slab
(excellent protection)

5c

5a

block stance

overhang section
(5b with 1 point of aid)

4b

obvious
deep chimney

big tree

small tree

tree stance

4b

root

4b

90 Pincushion

90 Barbarian

# 91: SCRATCH (VS) & SCRATCH ARÊTE (VS+) 60m

**Summary:** Popular climbs based on the right-hand slab of Peuterey Buttress. After an unremarkable start, Scratch quickly develops interest with a thought-provoking corner crack. Scratch Arête caps some fine slab climbing with a finger wrenching overhang. Adequate protection except on the first pitch of Scratch.

**First Ascent:** Scratch – A. J. J. Moulam and W. R. Craster, December 1953; Scratch Arête – B. Ingle and R. F. Jones, March 1962.

**Best Conditions:** Faces south at low altitude. The upper sections of both routes dry very quickly after rain; although the main crack on Scratch, and the first pitch of Scratch Arête, may remain damp for a little longer, particularly in winter.

**Approach:** As for Route 89.

**Starting Point:** Scratch: continue from the rock step as for Barbarian (Route 90) to the foot of the big corner (consider roping up for the 5m wall). Scratch Arête: at a tree about 10m right of the rock step.

**Descent:** Follow the path leftwards along the cliff top, rising uphill in places, to enter and descend a tree-filled recess on the left side of the main crag. A dilapidated wooden staircase provides rustic charm and occasional support.

The real interest on Scratch begins in a clean-cut corner above the half-way ledge. This poses a mixed jamming and laybacking problem of continuous, though never excessive, difficulty. Footholds of polished quartz allow occasional brief pauses to fix runners, but if things are going well it seems best not to interrupt the flow.

Excitement begins sooner on Scratch Arête – at a bulging crack just below the half-way ledge. Here founders the technician, while the thug steps over in triumph. Roles are reversed at the top overhang, so a party of mixed intelligence and ability will stand the best chance of overall success.

On the top pitch a slab of Pincushion-like delicacy delivers you below the stepped overhang with an irreversible semi-mantel. The position here, as the saying goes, leaves little to be desired. Unfortunately, the fingertip flakes used in surmounting the overhang leave a great deal to be desired. Small people must scrabble up using an inferior intermediate hold. Tall people simply yawn over the gap. There's no justice.

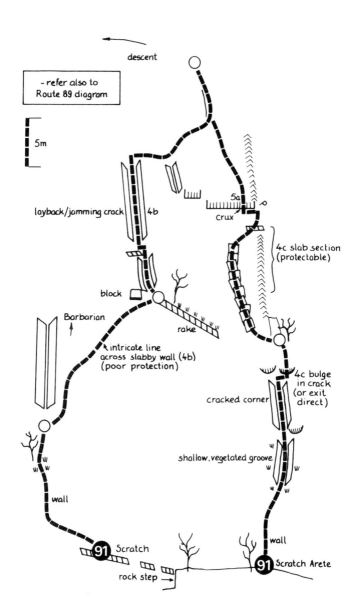

descent

- refer also to
Route 89 diagram

5m

layback/jamming crack    4b

5a
Crux

4c slab section
(protectable)

block

Barbarian

rake

intricate line
across slabby wall (4b)
(poor protection)

4c bulge
in crack
(or exit
direct)

cracked corner

shallow, vegetated groove

wall

wall

**91** Scratch

rock step →

**91** Scratch Arete

# 92: FALCON (E1) 60m

**Summary:** Face and crack climbing in concentrated form. Strenuous, protectable, intricate and private. A very desirable pitch.

**First Ascent:** R. James and M. Petrovsky, October 1962, as an aid route via its direct start. (Climbed free by J. Clements in 1964.)

**Best Conditions:** Faces south at low altitude. Dries quickly after rain, despite the cracks. Climbable at any time of year.

**Approach:** As for Route 89 to the boulder field. Try to identify the upper part of the route from here. An unattractive wall, disfigured by white blotches and black streaks, limits the left-hand side of the rightmost buttress on the crag. The slim corner of Vulcan, up which Falcon begins, defines the right side of this wall. Got It? Now enter the trees and follow a path to arrive, hopefully, at a small bay with a slabby rib to its left. 15mins.

**Descent:** (1) Traverse rightwards through dense undergrowth and descend the tree-filled recess on the right-hand side of the buttress. Take care, because the path ends abruptly above a hidden 15m wall! (Abseil).

(2) Struggle leftwards through equally dense, but more extensive, undergrowth to the top of the main crag. Descend as for Route 91.

Downward pointing spikes, the leading edge of a lowering portcullis, snatch at clothing as you layback out of the recessed stance. Cracks invite runners, but to pause is to falter, and to falter is to fail. An *in situ* peg a few metres higher brings no rest (except for the wicked), but does provide desperately needed security.

Here is the square-cut recess. A flat hold high on the right comes within reach, but a straight mantel is out of the question. Instead begins an extremely technical bridging sequence, finishing with an irreversible push across on to the hold. A rightward traverse from here is the only escape. Fingers settle on a crease, feet on a sliver, but then a blast of exposure hits you in the face like a shovel. No way! Calm down, think positive, try again. Have faith in rumours of hidden pockets!

A slight diversion avoids an initial steepening of the vertical fissure; but there's no dodging an awkward entry into a niche below overhangs, nor a bridging exit on tiring arms, nor a final wide crack, cruelly off-width. One pitch, six cruxes. Good value.

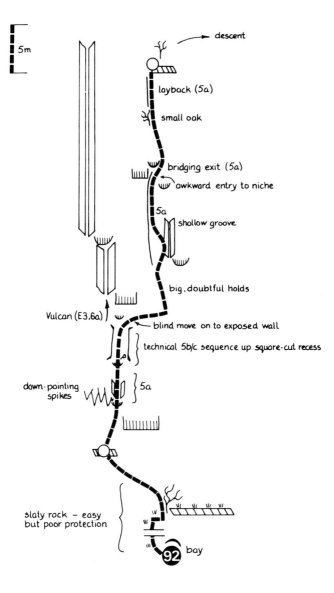

descent

layback (5a)

small oak

bridging exit (5a)

awkward entry to niche

5a

shallow groove

big, doubtful holds

Vulcan (E3,6a)

blind move on to exposed wall

technical 5b/c sequence up square-cut recess

down-pointing spikes

5a

slaty rock – easy but poor protection

**92** bay

5m

# 93: CHRISTMAS CURRY (S or S+) 75m & THE PLUM (E1) 45m

**Summary:** Varied climbing between spacious stances on Christmas Curry, the best of a small number of easier routes on this superb roadside crag. An optional finish up Micah Eliminate boosts grade and quality. The Plum confronts a succession of obstacles in its direct approach to the Micah arête.

**First Ascent:** Christmas Curry – A. J. J. Moulam and J. M. Barr, 25 December 1953 (Micah Finish – M. J. Harris, 1954); The Plum – R. James and D. Yates, December 1961.

**Best Conditions:** Faces south at low altitude and dries very quickly after rain. The first pitch of Christmas Curry can remain damp in winter or after prolonged rain.

**Approach:** From Bwlch y Moch Café on the A498 Beddgelert to Tremadog road (GR.575 405). Refer to Outlying Areas map for general location, and Coastal Areas map for details. Approach time less than 10mins.

**Starting Point:** Use the Route 95 crag diagram to help locate the upper part of the face. For Christmas Curry enter the jungle aiming for the lower right-hand side of the face. Start from a ledge and large tree below a chimney/gully line. For The Plum, climb the first pitch of Christmas Curry, and then scramble up to the right, to a tree belay below a corner capped by an overhang.

**Descent:** Down wooded slopes on the left side of the crag – awkward in places, especially when wet.

Newcomers to Tremadog must wonder what to make of this tree-shrouded outcrop with its car traffic, café, and perpetual sunshine. After wobbling up polished Ogwen classics in the rain, the climbing scene here must appear utterly decadent. Stick with it; it'll grow on you.

An assortment of insect and plant life on the early pitches of Christmas Curry add texture to a style of climbing that is uniquely Tremadog. The crucial entry to a scoop high on the top wall may be cleaner, but it's a lot less friendly. If you succeed on the original then be sure to return one day for Micah Eliminate, a superior variant which finishes in excellent position on a sharp arête.

Climbers on The Plum must battle through four distinct cruxes before arriving at the Micah arête: a layaway rib, blank groove, knee-jamming off-width, and a final friction move to gain the arête itself.

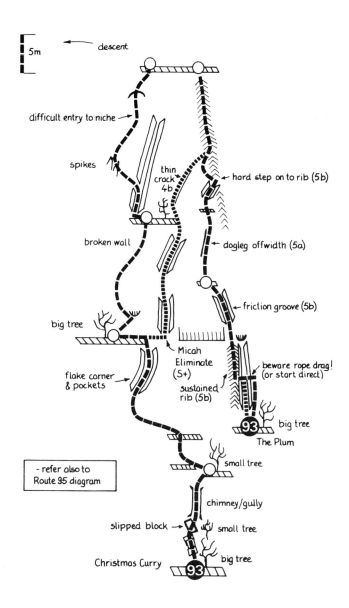

5m

descent

difficult entry to niche

spikes

thin crack 4b

hard step on to rib (5b)

broken wall

dogleg offwidth (5a)

friction groove (5b)

big tree

Micah Eliminate (S+)

beware rope drag! (or start direct)

flake corner & pockets

sustained rib (5b)

big tree

93 The Plum

- refer also to Route 95 diagram

small tree

chimney/gully

slipped block

small tree

Christmas Curry

big tree

93

# 94: THE FANG (HVS), EXTRACTION (E2) & STRIPTEASE (VS+) 60m

**Summary:** Three very different interpretations of a stubborn, tree-shrouded buttress. Poor protection plagues The Fang, which demands steadiness and careful ropework. Safer struggles characterise Striptease, while only the most imaginative runner techniques will ease the pain of Extraction.

**First Ascent:** Fang – J. Brown and C. E. Davies, June 1961; Extraction – C. J. Phillips and M. Crook, July 1975; Striptease – J. Brown and C. E. Davies, April 1961.

**Best Conditions:** Faces south at low altitude. Striptease stays remarkably dry, even after heavy showers. Conversely, the lower part of Fang may be found damp, especially in winter.

**Approach:** From Bwlch y Moch Café on the A498 Beddgelert to Tremadog road (GR.575 405). Refer to Outlying Areas map for general location, and Coastal Areas map for details. Approach time less than 10mins.

**Starting Point:** Use the Route 95 crag diagram to help locate the upper part of the buttress (note, in particular, the huge down-pointing spike of the Fang itself). A path leads with some scrambling directly to a ledge below Striptease corner. Fang starts up an undercut crack on a pinnacle to the left of the corner.

**Descent:** Down wooded slopes on the left side of the crag – awkward in places, especially when wet.

Striptease gets done on rainy days. It could be a myth that it stays dry, but Welsh weather guarantees its popularity. The crux reputedly arrives at a swing and pull-up near the top, but the polished exit from a lower niche is the real test.

A nice entry crack and wholesome layback are no preparation for the Fang traverse. The second, pinned to his tiny stance, risks being squashed like a grape by the unscheduled return of his brave leader. The top slab is easier, but there are few runners and many blind alleys. It seems to take a long time.

Extraction climbs up a thin, overhanging crack to the Fang stance. A high runner and side entry from the right seem sensible, but it will test nerve and stamina none the less. Its top pitch mirrors the Fang solution. An early baffling move to a ledge on the arête stops many leaders (clue: don't cross too high), and the return traverse is even harder. Most climbers only discover the hidden jug after completing the crucial move.

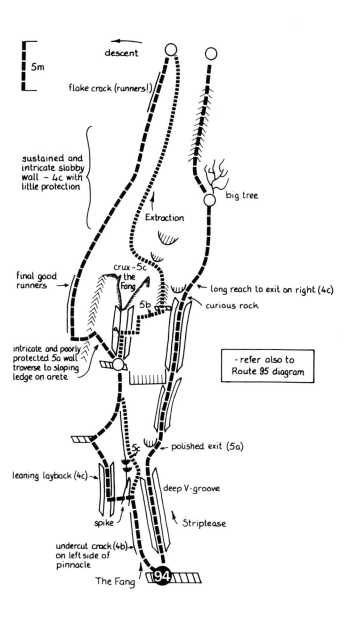

5m

descent

flake crack (runners!)

sustained and
intricate slabby
wall – 4c with
little protection

Extraction

big tree

final good
runners

crux – 5c
the Fang

long reach to exit on right (4c)

5b

curious rock

intricate and poorly
protected 5a wall
traverse to sloping
ledge on arete

- refer also to
Route 95 diagram

polished exit (5a)

5c

leaning layback (4c)

deep V-groove

Striptease

spike

undercut crack (4b)
on left side of
pinnacle

The Fang

94

# 95: ONE STEP IN THE CLOUDS (VS) 70m

**Summary:** Pleasant climbing on the left flank of Vector Buttress, raised from mediocrity by an excellent slabby rib. A popular, though far from ideal, introduction to roadside climbing at Tremadog. Adequate but spaced protection on the main pitch.

**First Ascent:** C. T. Jones and R. Moseley, May 1958.

**Best Conditions:** Faces south at low altitude. Climbable at any time of year. The upper part dries quickly after rain, but the lower pitches are sometimes damp.

**Approach:** From Bwlch y Moch Café on the A498 Beddgelert to Tremadog road (GR.575 405). Refer to Outlying Areas map for general location, and Coastal Areas map for details. Approach time less than 10mins.

**Starting Point:** Use the crag diagram opposite to help locate the upper part of the route. Aim to arrive at the lower right-hand side of the buttress, beneath impressive overhangs. Note the block-filled chimney on the left, which leads to a ledge and large tree at 10m.

**Descent:** Down wooded slopes on the left side of the crag – awkward in places, especially when wet.

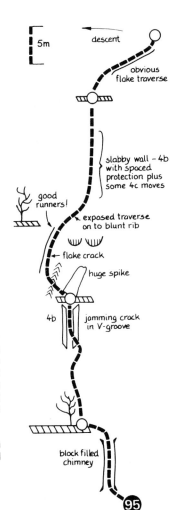

5m

descent

obvious
flake traverse

slabby wall – 4b
with spaced
protection plus
some 4c moves

good
runners!

exposed traverse
on to blunt rib

flake crack

huge spike

jamming crack
in V-groove

4b

block filled
chimney

95

descent

Tremadog –
Craig Bwlch y Moch

The name alone accounts for much of One Step's popularity; great
expectations animate the queues of climbers which gather here
each weekend. Make allowances for Trevor Jones's forgivable
moment of pretentiousness – or risk a pang of disappointment.

The route begins in typical Tremadog fashion with a steamy
chimney, deep within the green shade of the canopy. This looks
like solo territory, but an awkward lean and pads of lichen
persuade otherwise. A large tree secures the stance and offers a
grandstand view of the next pitch.

The V-groove seems to cause a lot of trouble. There is not much
to it, and the runners are good, but vigorous jamming is not to
everyone's taste. A fine stance by a huge spike eases tension.

A flake crack out left provides good jams and runners. From its
top a short leftward traverse would lead to an optional tree belay.
However, most leaders prefer to continue, trending rightwards on
to the undercut rib. This is the 'One Step' of repute: spaced
protection, balancy step-ups, breathtaking exposure. Aim to be
here during that transient phase in your climbing career between
inadequacy and indifference. You won't be disappointed.

# 96: VECTOR & THE WEAVER (E2) 75m

**Summary:** Joe Brown's intricate solution to the overhangs of Vector Buttress produced the best climb at Tremadog. Its reputation remains intact. Excellent protection, but only the determined will succeed. The Weaver seeks a more direct approach to the Vector Layback, visiting spectacular situations on the way.

**First Ascent:** Vector – J. Brown and C. E. Davies, March 1960; The Weaver – P. Williams and C. Shorter, February 1980.

**Best Conditions:** South-east facing at low altitude. Apart from the starting pitches, and the exit from the final layback, these routes rarely become saturated (a chalk trail on Vector remains visible throughout the year). During very

hot weather it may be worth waiting for late afternoon shade.

**Approach:** From Bwlch y Moch Café on the A498 Beddgelert to Tremadog road (GR.575 405). Refer to Outlying Areas map for general location, and Coastal Areas map for details. Approach time less than 10mins.

**Starting Point:** Use the Route 95 crag diagram to help locate the upper section (note the distinctive overhangs and streaked head wall). Aim to arrive at the lower right-hand side of the buttress (confirm position by identifying the Ochre Slab). Start by a large flake.

**Descent:** Down wooded slopes on the left side of the crag – awkward in places, especially when wet.

Vector is about mind control. A stretch move into a diagonal crack checks your credentials for some precarious wall moves above the big spike. An aid peg once delayed departure on the slippery, slanting blade of the Ochre Slab. Not any more. Bunched high on layaways the sequence begins at once, fingers clawing up the groove while feet skitter across its slabby right wall. The cave stance is bliss.

An intimidating overhang surrenders without a fight, the slab above likewise. The Weaver, meanwhile, is busy weaving a route up the bulging wall beneath, discovering holds and runners where none could be expected. They meet where a curving layback flake guards exit from the face. An initial pull up proves difficult, while the actual layback – in the Vector and Weaver context – feels comparatively secure. Late fallers, racked by last-minute uncertainty, join the long list of distinguished climbers cruelly plucked from its final move.

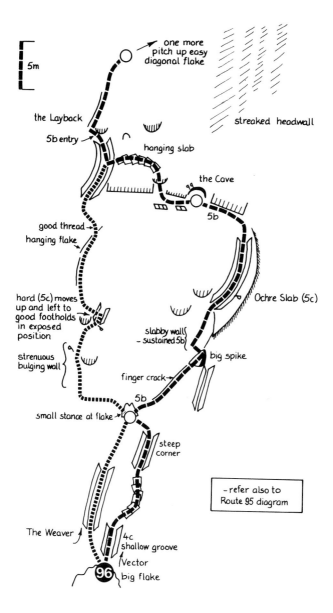

5m

one more
pitch up easy
diagonal flake

streaked headwall

the Layback

5b entry

hanging slab

the Cave

5b

good thread

hanging flake

Ochre Slab (5c)

hard (5c) moves
up and left to
good footholds
in exposed
position

slabby wall
– sustained 5b

big spike

strenuous
bulging wall

finger crack

5b

small stance at flake

steep
corner

– refer also to
Route 95 diagram

The Weaver

4c
shallow groove

Vector

96 big flake

# 97: MESHACH (VS+) & SHADRACH (VS) 60m

**Summary:** Aimless climbing on Meshach prolongs time spent on this wonderful slabby wall. Shadrach is more direct but initially less well protected. Two of the more popular climbs at Tremadog, and rightly so. Double ropes strongly recommended for Meshach.

**First Ascent:** Meshach – R. James, A. Earnshaw and M. Petrovsky, 1962; Shadrach – A. J. J. Moulam, G. W. S. Pigott and D. Thomas, May 1951.

**Best Conditions:** South facing at low altitude. The wall dries relatively quickly, although drainage streaks can affect Meshach. Idyllic on sunny, winter afternoons.

**Approach:** From Bwlch y Moch Café on the A498 Beddgelert to Tremadog road (GR.575 405). Refer to Outlying Areas map for general location, and Coastal Areas map for details. Approach time less than 10mins.

**Starting Point:** Use the Route 95 crag diagram to help locate the upper part of the wall. Aim to arrive at the lower left-hand side of the wall. A small slab guards a ledge which extends rightwards to a tree belay below the Shadrach chimney.

**Descent:** Down wooded slopes on the left side of the crag – awkward in places, especially when wet.

Three good climbs share a half-way stance on the left side of the wall. Meshach, the best of them, chooses the most indirect approach. At first, it follows a parallel line to Shadrach, enjoying safer but more difficult climbing on the open wall. But where the wall steepens, it darts down left, finding a hidden crack and ledge traverse leading to the half-way stance.

The main pitch shares Grim Wall's dynamic mantel before returning right, to enter a niche with a vicious pull on a finger flake. A peg runner now protects the crucial move right. Some do it high, others do it low. Statistics would reveal a better success potential among the 'lows' as they stride rightwards on to a hidden hold beneath the overlap. Isolated by that move, the head wall is sheer delight.

Shadrach's chimney is a nasty piece of work – inside or out (no ditherers outside, no helmets inside). A more dignified start takes the wide corner crack of The Brothers further right. Conventional wall climbing above ends on the pinnacle tip, from where a long reach and delicate foot change, to enter a slim corner, will prove crucial.

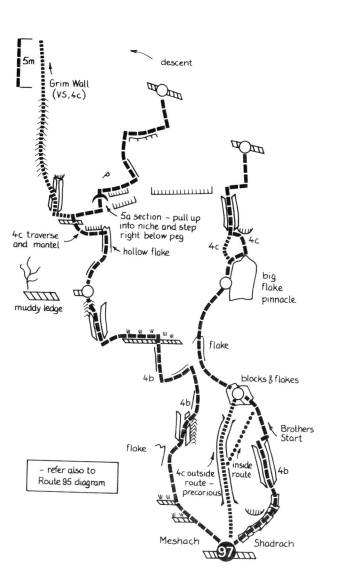

5m

Grim Wall
(VS, 4c)

descent

5a section – pull up
into niche and step
right below peg

4c traverse
and mantel

hollow flake

4c        4c

big
flake
pinnacle

muddy ledge

flake

4b

blocks & flakes

4b

Brothers
Start

flake

4c outside
route –
precarious

inside
route

4b

– refer also to
Route 95 diagram

Meshach

97

Shadrach

# 98: LEG SLIP (HVS) & FIRST SLIP (E1) 50m

**Summary:** Short, intense climbs of considerable technical difficulty: precarious friction bridging on First Slip; bold pull-ups on Leg Slip. Main difficulties are well protected.

**First Ascent:** J. Brown and C. E. Davies, March 1960.

**Best Conditions:** South facing at low altitude. Quick to dry after rain. However, both routes are affected by corner and overlap seepage after persistent rain. Otherwise, climbable at any time of year.

**Approach:** From Bwlch y Moch Café on the A498 Beddgelert to Tremadog road (GR.575 405).

Refer to Outlying Areas map for general location, and Coastal Areas map for details. Approach time less than 10mins.

**Starting Point:** Use the Route 95 crag diagram to help locate the upper section of the crag (note that these routes ascend the far right-hand side of Meshach wall). A path through trees leads directly towards the foot of the crag, finishing with a scramble to a tree stance below the shared initial groove.

**Descent:** Down wooded slopes on the left side of the crag – awkward in places, especially when wet.

The Slips share a common start in an undercut groove, where a dynamic entry commits you to a series of hurried layaway moves without proper rest. This sets the pace for all that follows. The two routes diverge at a corner capped by a roof: Leg Slip leftwards, gladly; First Slip upwards, reluctantly.

An unlikely ramp slices through overhangs and delivers Leg Slip at its crux – a compact V-corner. A flat hold on the right edge proves to be the key, but it takes nerve to swing out and up, abandoning all hope of retreat.

Back on First Slip the corner defeats all attempts at resting. Nothing for it but to set off hand traversing beneath the roof on shiny flat holds. After this, the first few moves of the crucial groove look positively inviting. Slot in a couple of runners and start bridging: dry rock, sticky boots, good protection – who needs holds?

You do. In one great final effort your left foot judders up on to a hold on the left wall. Relief. Now span the groove, reach up and clip the peg, push across towards the right edge, and teeter up to occupy the second best stance at Tremadog.

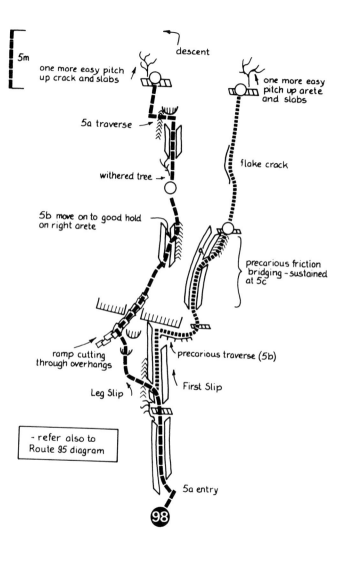

5m

descent

one more easy pitch
up crack and slabs

one more easy
pitch up arete
and slabs

5a traverse

flake crack

withered tree

5b move on to good hold
on right arete

precarious friction
bridging - sustained
at 5c

ramp cutting
through overhangs

precarious traverse (5b)

Leg Slip

First Slip

- refer also to
Route 95 diagram

5a entry

98

# 99: MERLIN (S) 60m & MERLIN DIRECT (VS+) 50m.

**Summary:** Contrasting climbs of quality on a detached roadside buttress next to the main Tremadog cliffs. The two routes share a mid-way stance and a layback crack, but little else. Good protection when it matters.

**First Ascent:** Merlin – A. J. J. Moulam and B. A. Jillott, April 1956; Merlin Direct – H. Smith and party, 1959.

**Best Conditions:** South facing at low altitude. The buttress drains quickly after rain, although trees will retard drying of the start and finish of the normal route. Climbable at any time of year.

**Approach:** From Bwlch y Moch Café on the A498 Beddgelert to Tremadog road (GR.575 405). Refer to Outlying Areas map for general location, and Coastal Areas map for details. Approach time less than 10mins.

**Starting Point:** Merlin Buttress stands very close to the road, isolated from the main crag by a vegetated break (confirm location by identifying the smooth 20m slab on its right side). Merlin starts at a huge block which leans against the toe of the buttress, the Direct on a pedestal adjacent to the smooth slab.

**Descent:** Via Belshazzar Gully on the left side of the buttress (some scrambling).

The rocks on Merlin Buttress are not the most stable at Tremadog. Its central bay collapses *en masse* every few years, while individual flakes and blocks detach themselves sporadically from the more solid flanks – sometimes with a climber attached. A recent departure was the starting flake of Merlin, which left a *6a* groove in its place. That would never do, so an alternative start was found to bypass the difficulty – though not without some increase in standard. Hence this rearrangement of the two routes.

After a promising start Merlin resigns itself to plodding up grassy slabs. This leads to a tree stance which is supported, for the time being, by a pile of blocks. Those following the Direct must expect to work harder to reach the same place.

A delicate step gains the shared layback. The term is merely a convenience, because footholds and hand jams render it harmless. The routes diverge at an overlap: the original to friction rightwards and enter a shady corner; the Direct to traverse deviously left and finish magnificently up the head wall.

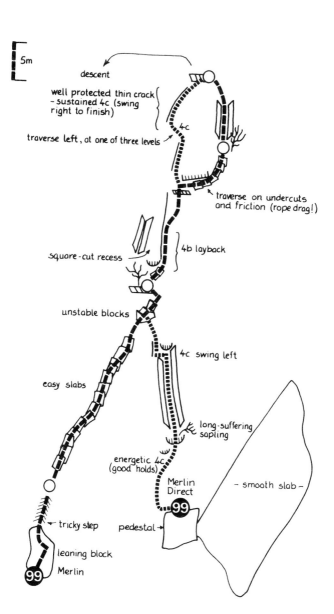

5m

descent

well protected thin crack – sustained 4c (swing right to finish)

4-c

traverse left, at one of three levels

traverse on undercuts and friction (rope drag!)

4b layback

square-cut recess

unstable blocks

4c swing left

easy slabs

long-suffering sapling

energetic 4c (good holds)

Merlin Direct

99

pedestal

smooth slab

tricky step

leaning block

Merlin

99

# 100: HARDD (E1) 50m & HYLLDREM GIRDLE (VS+) 70m

**Summary:** Incredible climbing among the overhangs of a brutal outcrop. Sound rock of slaty texture. Adequate protection for the hardest moves. Both routes demand capable seconds.

**First Ascent:** Hardd – J. Brown, G. D. Roberts and N. Drasdo, March 1960; Hylldrem Girdle – J. Brown and G. D. Verity, March 1960.

**Best Conditions:** South-east facing at low altitude. Quick to dry after rain. Drainage streaks may affect Hardd after prolonged bad weather. Bands of overhangs shelter the main part of the Girdle from rain. Climbable at any time of year.

**Approach:** From Beddgelert follow the A498 south for 2km to Abergaslyn Bridge, and then turn left on the A4085 towards Penrhyndeudraeth. After about 5km there is a sharp right bend over a bridge; the crag towers above the road just before this bend at GR.615 431. Refer to Outlying Areas map for general location. Roadside parking for several cars.

**Starting Point:** Girdle – at a large tree below the main wall on the right-hand side of the crag. Hardd – ascend a ramp rightwards from the tree to a small stance (confirm location by identifying the distinctive isolated bulge about 8m above).

**Descent:** Via wooded slopes well to the right of the crag.

There are no easy routes here. More often than not the first visit is made in a bid to escape unexpected rain at Tremadog. Ugly little Hylldrem has no devotees of its own.

The Girdle lives up to its reputation as an all-weather route. An umbrella of overhangs shields it even from torrential rain.

Hardd sets about the main wall in defiant mood. A peg move on the initial wall now goes free, though not for the impatient. However, purist and pragmatist alike will arrive flustered at the bulge. Here a runner protects an irreversible foot slide to the left – the first of two trying moves on this crucial traverse. Some leaders pluck up courage to make the first, but not the second. Sadly for them, this is one job that can't be left half done!

Despite all this effort the route actually gets nowhere, stranded on a little ledge among bulging rock. No alternative but to abseil down over an overhang, swing across to regain rock, and hand traverse out of trouble. Obvious really.

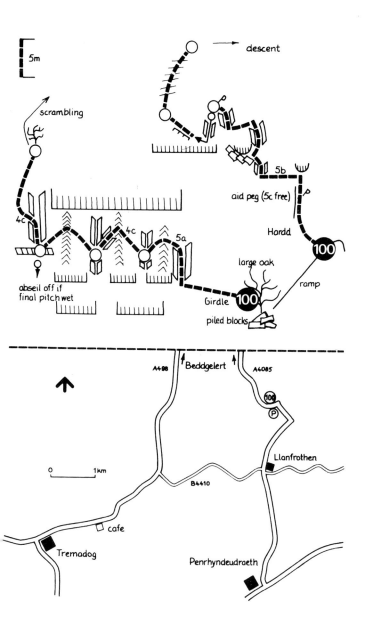

## Also in the Crowood Classic Climbs series:

Scotland (Central and Southern Highlands)
The Lake District
Peak and Pennines (Gritstone)